Contactees

Contactees

A History of
Alien-Human Interaction

Nick Redfern

New
Page
BOOKS

The Career Press, Inc.
Franklin Lakes, N.J.

CONTACTEES
EDITED BY KATE HENCHES
TYPESET BY GINA TALUCCI
Cover design by Howard Grossman/12E Design
Printed in the U.S.A. by Courier

To order this title, please call toll-free 1-800-CAREER-1 (NJ and Canada: 201-848-0310) to order using VISA or MasterCard, or for further information on books from Career Press.

The Career Press, Inc., 3 Tice Road, PO Box 687,
Franklin Lakes, NJ 07417
www.careerpress.com
www.newpagebooks.com

Dedication

For Greg, a fine friend and an inspiration.

And in memory of Mac Tonnies, a friend whose flame was extinguished all too soon.

Acknowledgments

I would like to offer my very sincere thanks to the following people, without whom the writing and publication of this book would never have been possible:

My literary agent, Lisa Hagan, whose dogged persistence ensured that the book saw the light of day; Michael Pye, Laurie Kelly-Pye, Kirsten Dalley, Kate Henches, Gina Talucci, and everyone at Career Press and New Page Books for their hard work and enthusiasm; Kate Warwick-Smith and all at Warwick Associates for promoting *Contactees*; Greg Bishop, who is truly one of today's most informed researchers of the Contactee mystery, and who was highly generous with his time and data; Mac Tonnies (who tragically died just before this book was published) for the interview, and for delving into an area of the UFO subject that few have dared to investigate; Micah Hanks, for the illuminating data he provided on the mysterious Brown Mountain Lights, DMT, and much more; Adam Gorightly, whose views on, and knowledge of, the era of the Space-Brothers have always been very welcome and thought-provoking; Timothy Green Beckley, for taking the time out of his busy schedule to share with me his memories, ideas, and thoughts on the Contactees; Jim Moseley, long-time observer of the UFO scene, whose stories about his encounters with the early Contactees were a pleasure to hear; Regan Lee, for her generosity in sharing her research, and for continuing to fly the flag of Dana Howard; Rich Reynolds, a man with a lot to say about UFOs, and who isn't afraid to say it, for allowing me to make use of one of the strangest of all stories from his voluminous files; Matthew Williams, for being willing to speak to me about his views on the Crop Circle mystery; Chris Bader, for his enthusiasm, and for loaning me some invaluable material on the Contactees; Bob Short, for the interview and for continuing to keep the flame of the Space-Brothers alight; and Colin Bennett for his lengthy, enlightening, and illuminating views, opinions, and observations on Adamski, Williamson, and all the rest of that heady bunch known collectively as the Contactees.

Contents

Introduction

The era of the flying saucer was ushered in on June 24, 1947, when a pilot named Kenneth Arnold had an extraordinary airborne encounter at the Cascade Mountains, Washington State, USA. It was around 3.00 p.m. and Arnold was engaged in looking for an airplane that had crashed on the southwest side of Mt. Rainier. "I hadn't flown more than two or three minutes on my course when a bright flash reflected on my airplane," said Arnold. "It startled me as I thought I was too close to some other aircraft. I looked every place in the sky and couldn't find where the reflection had come from until I looked to the left and the north of Mt. Rainier, where I observed a chain of nine peculiar looking aircraft flying from north to south at approximately 9,500 feet elevation and going, seemingly, in a definite direction of about 170 degrees" (Palmer, 1952).

Arnold added that the mysterious crafts were closing in rapidly on Mt. Rainier, and that he was highly puzzled by their overall design: "I thought it was very peculiar that I couldn't find their tails but assumed they were some type of jet plane. The more I observed these objects, the more upset I became, as I am accustomed and familiar with most all objects flying whether I am close to the ground or at higher altitudes. The chain of these saucer-like objects [was] at least five miles long. I felt confident that after I would land, there would be some explanation of what I saw [sic]" (Ibid.).

No firm conclusion for Arnold's encounter ever did surface; however, as the skies of the United States became populated with more and more flying saucers during the heady summer of 1947, the United States military quickly realized that finding an answer to the mystery was an issue of paramount importance. As a result, investigations were put into place, and which became unified under the banner of an official operation named *Project Sign*. In 1948, *Sign* was replaced by *Project Grudge*, which, in turn, became *Project Blue Book*—the latter being the Air Force's most famous and publicly visible UFO study program. It continued until 1969, when it was finally closed down.

Although the Air Force grudgingly admitted that of the 12,618 reports it had investigated between 1947 and 1969, no less than 701 seemingly defied definitive explanation, military officials were adamant that no evidence existed in support of the notion that alien beings were visiting the Earth. But perhaps the Air Force's apparent inability to resolve the matter was because the phenomenon did not behave in a fashion that its personnel might have anticipated or expected of them. There was never any *War of the Worlds* or *Independence Day*–style invasion of the planet; and human beings were not secretly replaced by alien look-a-likes, in some macabre, real-life version of *Invasion of the Body Snatchers*. But, equally, there was no friendly, historic touch-down of an extra-terrestrial vehicle on the lawns of the White House, in the grounds of Buckingham Palace, or outside the doors of the Kremlin.

Indeed, there are reasons for believing that those whose role it was to protect the free world from hostile invaders were seemingly looking for the aliens in all the wrong places: While the military was dispatching its jets to chase flying saucers in the skies above, or scanning its radar screens for evidence of unknown objects violating sensitive airspace, it was at ground-level that remarkable things were reportedly afoot.

Since the late 1940s, countless people, all across the world, have claimed face-to-face contact with eerily human-like aliens from far-off planets. The aliens in question are usually seen dressed in tight-fitting, one-piece-outfits, while sporting heads of lush, long, and flowing blond hair. Not only that, our cosmic visitors assure those of us who they deem worthy of contact that they are deeply concerned by our warlike ways. They wish us to disarm our nuclear arsenals, live in peace and harmony with one another, and elevate ourselves to whole new spiritual levels. The aliens in question have become known as the Space-Brothers; those whose lives have been touched and forever changed by their encounters with such alleged extra-terrestrial entities are an elite body of people known as the Contactees.

If the testimony of the witnesses can be considered valid, then in the early years of contact the aliens took a decidedly alternative approach to their liaisons with the people of Earth, something that may explain why the military had such a hard time proving the reality of the UFO phenomenon. Allegedly preferring face-to-face encounters with everyday members of society, the Space-Brothers arranged their clandestine meetings at such out-of-the-way locations as blisteringly hot deserts, dense forests, stark mountain peaks, and even within isolated diners situated on long stretches of dusty, sand and wind-blasted highway. And California was a particularly favorite haunt and haven of the Space-Brothers, too.

Moreover, in many cases on record, the aliens did not even greet their elite, chosen ones in glistening, futuristic spacecraft. Rather, exhibiting surprisingly good taste and a high degree of flair and panache, in the formative years of contact they sometimes preferred far more conventional forms of travel, including cool-looking cars of the type that dominated 1950s America. This book tells the collective, curious, and cosmic story in all its appropriately weird wonder.

1

Early Encounters

Although there can be no doubt that it was during the early to late 1950s that all-things of a Contactee nature dominated the world of flying saucers, a few earlier encounters were reported. One such case can be found in the declassified UFO files of the FBI. The story began on July 9, 1949, when columnist Walter Winchell brought to the attention of J. Edgar Hoover a story he had received from a "Mr. Jones of Los Angeles" who maintained he had seen a flying saucer in the summer of 1947. Winchell advised Hoover that Jones had mailed him a letter that was "very well written, obviously by a man of intelligence" (Winchell, 1949).

In view of this, the FBI took time out to pursue the matter, as the following memorandum, written by FBI Assistant Director D.M. Ladd shows:

> In this letter, Jones stated that in August of 1947 he left Los Angeles for the mountains and started hiking through the mountains. About 10:00 a.m. he was laying on the ground when he observed about one-half block away from him a large, silver, metal object, greenish in color, shaped like a child's top and about the size of the balloons used at country fairs.
>
> He stated that there appeared to be two windows in the object and portions of metal appeared transparent and that he gained the impression that there was some life within this object although he saw no persons. The object appeared as though sealed as a pressure chamber. He stood up and waved toward this object and this

so-called flying saucer was off the ground in a second, knocking Jones to the ground. In its flight he stated that its power was silent and he raised the question as to whether this was an inter-global landing on our planet. He thought that it might be a device to land on our planet because the occupants of another planet had become curious as to the reaction caused by the atomic bomb causing trouble in an expanding universe. He asked the question as to whether it was possible that the occupants of another planet might have solved the theory of negative energy (FBI, 1949).

A source whose name has been excised from the FBI files—but who was described as having a scientific background—advised the Bureau that Jones's communication suggested he possessed a very good knowledge of physics, and added it might be to the FBI's advantage to check into Jones's background and interview him at the earliest opportunity. All attempts to do so were unsuccessful, however: Jones could not be located, or had seemingly vanished. There are, however, a couple of issues that are worthy of note.

First: Jones reportedly lived in California—just like many of the original Contactees. Second: As was the case with many who followed in his path, Jones's encounter occurred in a remote location. Then, there is the matter of the concern exhibited by the aliens in relation to the power of the atom. Was this merely a case of Jones speculating? If so, it was an astonishing coincidence: Only a few years later countless other people were making very similar observations of an atomic kind.

Furthermore, that Jones's encounter occurred in the mountains while he was laying on the ground, raises an important question: Was Jones in some form of altered state of mind throughout his encounter, and perhaps one brought on by the occupants of the strange, aerial device? If that was the case, then Jones' story may possibly represent one of the earliest Contactee cases on record. As will become clear later, however, there are indications that the Contactee phenomenon may actually be a very ancient one, and one in which altered states play a vital role.

Born in Township, Minnesota, in 1908, Daniel William Fry claimed a close encounter of the alien kind at the White Sands Proving Ground, New Mexico: He asserted he took a flight in an extraterrestrial spacecraft—on Independence Day, 1949, no less—to New York and back in barely half-an-hour! So the story went, Fry intended to celebrate the holiday period with colleagues from the base in the town of Las Cruces. Unfortunately, he missed the bus and was forced to remain on-base—alone. So, instead, he decided to do a bit of exploring in the vast expanse of desert that makes up what is, today, called the White Sands Missile Range. It's highly unlikely that Fry ever anticipated coming into contact with a being from another world while he roamed the isolated area, and yet that is precisely what he said happened.

"I headed first in the direction of the old static test stand, on which we were mounting our largest rocket motor," reported Fry. "About two thirds of the way to the test stand, a small dirt road intersects [with] the main road, and leads off to the right toward the base of the Organ Mountains" (Fry, 1992).

He added: "Directly ahead of me, and just over the peaks of the Organ Mountains, an especially bright group of stars seemed to beckon to me as I walked leisurely along. Then, suddenly, the brightest of the stars simply went out...something I could not see was eclipsing the light of the star" (Ibid.).

Fry soon found out what that "something" was.

Out of the skies descended "a spheroid, considerably flattened at the top and bottom. The vertical dimension was about 16 feet, and the horizontal dimension about 30 feet at the widest point...if viewed from directly below it might appear to be saucer shaped, but actually it was more nearly like a soup bowl inverted over a sauce dish" (Ibid.).

As Fry looked on ("as a child might stare at the rabbit which a stage magician has just pulled from his hat"), a disembodied voice that went by the name of A-lan told Fry that the device appearing before him was being remotely controlled by a "mother-ship" orbiting the planet at a height of around 900 miles (Ibid.). Then there came a bombshell-style question: Would Fry like to take a ride across the country in the craft? Of course, he would! He was supposedly whisked across the night sky to New York and back in no more than half an hour. The journey may not have been long; but it was significant. While Fry was on board, the voice of A-lan related a wealth of data relative to the forgotten history of humanity:

"Tens of thousands of years ago, some of our ancestors lived upon this planet, Earth. There was, at that time, a small continent in a part of the

The White Sands Missile Range—the scene of Daniel
Fry's alien encounter. Courtesy of Nick Redfern.

now sea-covered area which you have named the Pacific Ocean. Some of
your ancient legends refer to this sunken land mass as the 'Lost Continent
of Lemuria or Mu.' Our ancestors had built a great empire and mighty
science upon this continent. At the same time, there was another rapidly
developing race upon a land mass in the southwestern portion of the
present Atlantic Ocean. In your legends, this continent has been named
Atlantis" (Challenor, 2001).

According to A-lan, "increasing bitterness" between the two cultures, as
well as "their constantly increasing command of destructive energies," led to
a catastrophic war. He explained to Fry: "...the resulting nuclear radiation
was so intense and so widespread, that the entire surface became virtually
unfit for habitation, for a number of generations." Before departing, and
in a fashion that would become typical of the Space-Brothers, A-lan gave

Fry a message pertaining to the potential for atomic disaster that faced humankind: "As nuclear weapons proliferate among your nations, it should always be remembered that an ounce of understanding is worth a megaton of deterrent'" (Ibid.).

In essence, that is Daniel Fry's tale. But what should we make of it? It's worth noting that Fry's interest in rocketry was formulated in his youth, and his undoubtedly skilled work at White Sands was with the prestigious company Aerojet. Based out of Sacramento, California, Aerojet is today the only United States–based body to provide both solid-rocket and liquid-rocket engines, and has the contract to provide nearly all the U.S. Army's tactical-missile rocket-motors. In other words, to have been employed by such a company, Fry had to have something in his favor. But, there were a few problems.

In 1954, shortly after going public with his story, Fry flunked a lie-detector test, and it was later learned that his much-flaunted "doctorate," bestowed upon him around early 1960, had actually been obtained via a London, England, mail-order organization called the Saint Andrews College. This did not stop Fry from developing a large following of like-minded individuals, however. From 1954 onward, Fry delivered numerous lectures across the United States; one year later, established a group called Understanding Inc. that helped spread the word of the Space-Brothers.

Such was the interest in Fry's claims of alien contact that Understanding Inc. went on to publish a monthly newsletter that ran for 23 years: Nearly 250 issues were published between 1956 and 1979. Moreover, at its height, in the early 1960s, Understanding Inc. boasted almost 1,500 members, and became the recipient of 55-acres of land near Tonopah, Arizona, that had been donated by a Reverend Enid Smith. The irony of this was that the buildings, first intended by Smith to act as a religious college, were shaped like classic flying saucers. Understanding, Inc. took full control of the property in 1976; however, with membership falling, the site ultimately fell into disrepair. In late September and early October 1978, the kitchen and library were burned to the ground by an arsonist and were never rebuilt. Further tragedy followed: One year later, Fry's second wife, Florence, died from breast cancer—he had divorced wife number one, Elma, in 1964. Although Fry's place within the annals of UFOlogy was largely over by the dawning of the 1980s, he continued to give the occasional lecture and interview, before ultimately passing on in December 1992—still standing by his every assertion of that long gone, July 4, 1949, night when he soared across the starlit skies of the United States, with nothing but an intergalactic, disembodied voice for company.

Let us now turn to the controversial story of Samuel Eaton Thompson, who claimed an encounter in March 1950, that certainly set the scene for a whole range of similar tales that would soon follow in its bizarre wake. Respected UFO authority Jerome Clark has justifiably described Thompson's story as "surely the most outlandish story in early UFO history [and] also one of the most obscure" (Clark, 1998).

That the tale surfaced on April Fools' Day in 1950, has led some commentators to suspect that Thompson's claims were merely borne out of a good-natured prank; others, meanwhile, are not quite so certain that fakery was a dominating factor. As Thompson told the story, on the night of March 28, 1950, he was driving between the towns of Morton and Mineral, Washington State; he had been visiting relatives in Markham and was headed towards his Centralia home. Tired, and needing a break, Thompson pulled his vehicle over to the side of the road in a heavily-wooded area, and took a walk along a nearby logging trail. He was shocked to the core by the scene upon which he stumbled.

As he reached a clearing in the trees, Thompson maintained that sat before him was a large object, "shaped liked two saucers fused together," that was around 80 feet in width, 30 feet in height, and hovering very slightly above the forest floor. Two naked and heavily sun-tanned, human-like children were blissfully playing near the entrance to the craft, which could be accessed via a small ramp. Thompson added that as he got to within about 50 feet of the craft, he felt extremely hot, at which point several adults—humanoid, "attractive," and also naked—appeared in the doorway of the strange object. When Thompson succeeded in convincing them that he meant no harm, they invited him aboard what he quickly deduced was an alien spacecraft, but not before being made to remove his shoes and socks (*Centralia Daily Chronicle*, 1950).

Thompson learned from the crew—who spoke in a stilted form of English—that there were 20 adults and 25 children aboard the craft, who originated on the planet Venus, and that this was not merely a space vessel: It was their home, too, as they adventurously explored the solar system.

Strangely, as Jerome Clark noted when commenting on Thompson's recollections, the entities seemed to operate "more by instinct than by intellect" (Clark, 1998). As Thompson watched the aliens' actions, he noted that, although they understood which levers to pull and which buttons to press to operate their craft, it was all done parrot-fashion and without any actual understanding of their actions.

Evidently, this didn't bother Thompson: He claimed to have spent 40 hours romping around the ship—during which time he learned a great deal, such as the revelation that several of their craft had been shot down by military forces on Earth and that everyone of humankind's problems stemmed from astrology, and specifically because human beings were born under a variety of star-signs (which always led to conflict), whereas Venusians were all born under the sign of—what else?—Venus. And Thompson seemed to accept, quite matter-of-factly, the startling assertions of the aliens that he, Thompson, was nothing less than a fully fledged, reincarnated Venusian! Thompson was also told that the aliens were vegetarian, enjoyed excellent health, and desired to help us by ushering in a new era of humanity that would culminate in a return to our planet by Jesus Christ in 10,000 AD.

According to Thompson, he remained on the spaceship until March 30th. He did admit, however, that at one point he quickly returned home to get his camera, so that he might capture the moment on film for posterity. The photographs came out as either "just blank" or as mere blobs of light. Before he finally left for good, Thompson was given a friendly warning by his cosmic friends that he should keep certain information strictly confidential. Whether or not the aliens were impressed by Thompson's decision to spill the interplanetary beans to the *Centralia Daily Chronicle* on April 1st is unknown. However, because Thompson was not blessed with a return visit from the Venusians, we might correctly assume they were hardly cheered by his decision to blow the whistle on their actions.

There is an interesting sequel to this odd affair: After Thompson's story hit the headlines, none other than Kenneth Arnold interviewed Thompson. He concluded that Thompson was not a purveyor of fakery. Rather, he believed the man had undergone some form of psychic experience—"whatever that actually means," as Jerome Clark wryly commented (Clark, 1998). Many people would simply relegate Thompson's odd, and frankly unbelievable, tale to the garbage can, and maybe their actions would be justified. Yet, such similar tales literally abound within the domain of the Contactees. What might be the root cause of Thompson's report, and a number of very similar ones, becomes much clearer later.

2

The Ultimate Contactee

George Adamski was born on April 17, 1891, in Poland, and claimed sensational alien encounters in the California desert in the early 1950s—the details of which were told in the packed pages of a controversial, 1953 blockbuster-book co-authored with British writer Desmond Leslie, titled *Flying Saucers Have Landed*. Before we get deep into things of a long-haired and saucer-shaped variety as they relate to Adamski, let's start at the beginning. At the age of 2, Adamski and his family moved to the United States and put down roots in New York. From 1913 to 1916, he served in the military; then, one year later, moved west, began working at Yellowstone National Park, and later took employment at an Oregon-based flour mill. But the normality of everyday life was not for Adamski. While in Laguna Beach in the 1930s, he founded the Royal Order of Tibet. In other words, long before the relocated Pole maintained he met long-haired aliens in the deserts of California, he was already delving into a lifestyle that some might have seen as alternative.

An article that appeared in the *LA Times* in April 1934 titled "Shamanistic Order to be Established Here" offered an illuminating insight into the life of Adamski: "The 10-foot trumpets of far away Lhasa, perched among perpetual snows in the Himalayan Mountains in Tibet, will shortly have their echo on the sedate hills of Souther California's Laguna Beach. Already the Royal Order of Tibet has acquired acreage on the placid hills that bathe their Sunkist feet in the purling Pacific and before long, the walls, temples, turrets and dungeons of a Lama monastery will serrate the skyline. It will be the first Tibetan monastery in America and in course of time, the trained disciples of the cult will filter through its glittering gates to spread 'the ancient truths' among all who care to listen. [The] central figure in the new movement is Prof. George Adamski" (*LA Times*, 1934).

"'I learned great truths up there on the roof of the world,' says Adamski, 'or rather the trick of applying age-old knowledge to daily life, to cure the body and the mind, and to win mastery over self and soul. I do not bring to Laguna the weird rites and bestial superstition in which the old Lamaism is steeped, but the scientific portions of the religion'" (Ibid.).

Six years later, Adamski moved yet again—with a group of friends to a ranch near California's Palomar Mountain. Then, in 1944, the group purchased 20 acres of land on Palomar Mountain, constructed a new home called Palomar Gardens, and opened a restaurant called the Palomar Gardens Café. It wasn't too long before Adamski's life became distinctly weird. On October 9, 1946, Adamski and a number of his buddies claimed that while they were at the Palomar Gardens' campground, they saw a huge cigar-shaped UFO. One year later, Adamski photographed the very same craft, once again at Palomar Gardens. Other sightings of apparently unidentified aerial vehicles followed, but Adamski's true crowning glory came in the final weeks of 1952.

Greg Bishop, one of the leading authorities on the Contactee controversy, tells the story:

...Adamski left his Palomar mountain retreat at 1 a.m. on Thursday November 20, 1952 along with his lifetime secretary Lucy McGinnis and Alice Wells—the owner of the property where Adamski gave lectures on Universal Law and the café where he flipped burgers to pay the rent. At about 8 a.m. they met with Al Bailey and his wife Betty, and George Hunt Williamson [a fellow-Contactee] and his wife, Betty, in Blythe, [California] just west of the Arizona/California border.

Turning back on a 'hunch' the group retraced their drive back to Desert Center and took a small highway 11 miles northeast towards the town of Parker, Arizona and stopped. After a meal, the group aimlessly scanned the skies for saucers. Passing motorists slowed to rubberneck at this small band staring into the sky in the middle of a barren desert. Shortly after noon, a plane passed overhead, causing momentary excitement. The real drama began moments later, when 'riding high and without sound, there was a gigantic cigar-shaped silvery ship.'

Williamson understatedly asked: 'Is that a space ship?' as Betty Bailey tried to set up a movie camera, but couldn't because 'she was so excited.' According to Adamski, they were anxious not to attract attention to the object, so they didn't point at it and alert other passing cars to this event.

'Someone take me down the road, quick! That ship has come looking for me and I don't want to keep them waiting!' Adamski yelled, and jumped into the car with McGinnis and Mr. Bailey. About a half-mile down the road, with the craft shadowing them, Adamski told McGinnis to turn off the road. He then instructed the two to 'go back to the others as quickly as possible…and watch for anything that might take place'—from the safe viewing distance of half a mile or more away. After this first craft was chased away by interceptor jets, another 'beautiful small craft' arrived and landed behind the crest of a mountain about half a mile away.

Soon, he saw a figure waving to him and walked towards it. Suddenly Adamski 'fully realized I was in the presence of a man from space—a being from another world!' Adamski learned [the being] was from Venus and that his name was Orthon. After some warnings about atomic weapons and wars, and a refusal to be photographed, he returned to his ship and sailed away.

Adamski waved to his companions to approach, which they did soon after. Conveniently enough Williamson had brought along some plaster-of-paris and proceeded to make casts of the footprints the Venusian had left in the desert floor. According to Williamson…he was 'the first to arrive at the footprints after the contact had been made. I could see where the space being had scraped away the topsoil in order to get more moist sand that would take the impressions from the carvings on the bottom of his shoes. The carvings on the shoes must have been finely done for the impressions in the sand were clear cut.'

Either Orthon had a weight problem on Earth, or someone had taken extra care in making the impressions. He goes on to state his interpretation of what meaning the symbols hold for those who 'fail to obey the laws of the Infinite Father.' Williamson also stresses that the designs are not 'alien,' because the Earth is 'part of the Great Totality' and ancient symbols of Earth are the symbols of the space beings as well…after this event Williamson seemed to have found his calling, and concentrated on turning out his own brand of Contactee literature—most of it 'channeled'—leaving clear the nuts-and-bolts domain to his friend and inspiration, the other George—Adamski (Bishop, 2000).

Before continuing with the saga of Adamski, a tad more data is required on George Hunt Williamson—who was an integral part of Adamski's most sensational claims. Also known as Michael d'Obrenovic and Brother Philip, Williamson was born in Chicago, Illinois, in 1926, became entranced by the occult in his teens, and evolved into a significant player on the saucer scene of the 1950s. In early 1951 Williamson was thrown out of the University of Arizona; however, having read and been deeply influenced by William Dudley Pelley's 1950 book *Star Guests*, he subsequently helped produce the group's monthly publication, *Valor*.

At the time, Pelley had been recently released from prison after serving eight years for his wartime opposition to President Roosevelt. The leader of a definitively fascist group known as the *Silver Shirts*, Pelley, just like Williamson, was fascinated by occult matters and compiled massive volumes of "automatic writing" on contact with allegedly higher forms of intelligence. Pelley became a major influence on the life of Williamson—who ultimately combined his fascination with the occult and flying saucers by trying to contact extraterrestrial-intelligences with a homemade Ouija board. Upon learning of some of the early assertions of George Adamski, Williamson became a regular visitor to Adamski's commune, which is what led to his presence at Adamski's encounter with Orthon.

In 1954, Williamson and the aforementioned Al Bailey published their own saucer-dominated volume: *The Saucers Speak*, which focused upon Williamson's attempts to contact extraterrestrials via the alternative mediums of short-wave radio and Ouija-boards. Actar of Mercury; Adu

The planet Venus—the alleged home of Orthon the extraterrestrial. Photo courtesy of NASA.

of Hatonn in Andromeda; Agfa Affa from the dark depths of Uranus; Ankar-22 of Jupiter; Artok of Pluto; and numerous others were among the motley alien crew with whom Williamson claimed to have communicated. In the late 1950s, Williamson changed his name, created a new fictitious academic and family background to accompany his latest moniker, and—as far as the Contactee issue was concerned—largely vanished. Williamson died in 1986, a figure by then largely forgotten, or completely unknown to the UFO research community of the day. Adamski, meanwhile, was a player on the saucer scene right up until the time he took his very last breath.

On the matter of the relationship between Adamski and Williamson, researcher Colin Bennett states:

Adamski was not an educated man, and he used the better-educated Williamson as he used Desmond Leslie, that is as an extra cerebral lung. As such, George Hunt Williamson was the top of Adamki's multi-media head. As they used to say in those days, they both tripped one another out. The Mojave was certainly rich in ancient Indian legends concerning flying vehicles. This was one of the reasons why George Hunt Williamson and the Baileys accompanied Adamski to the desert. It is more than possible that the group wanted to conjure up something like the kind of presence that they thought they had contacted from their automatic writing, and at least Adamski got more than he bargained for. A combination of high intrigue, burgeoning exotic technology combined with the ancient desert and its prehistoric features was not to be trifled with, and a genie came right of the alchemical bottle. All the best books on occultism contain the warning that the attempted raising of images is not to be taken lightly.

It is important to understand that like Alan Ginsberg and Jack Kerouac, both Adamski and Williamson were fully inspired by the birth of this brave new world. It threaded through them as ivy threads through a house if it is not cut off; and neither Adamski nor Williamson were the kind of men to cut off any kind of speculative growth. Prototypal belief-systems sprouted almost from the top of their heads, and surreal conspiracies were the very breath of their being. Both were breathless Americans in the first nuclear age, and both were as excited as rich kids let loose in a big-city toyshop (Bennett, 2009).

There is another issue that requires comment: in 1949 Adamski penned a little-known sci-fi novel titled *Pioneers of Space* that told a story suspiciously similar to those which he later began presenting as fact. Timothy Green Beckley, who, in 2009, published a new edition of *Pioneers of Space*, concedes that there are indeed similarities between Adamski's novel and his later, allegedly non-fiction titles on flying saucers, but qualifies this with the following:

"It can be theorized, and this is what I believe, that [Adamski's] mental attitude was the proper one for him to be drawn into an alien encounter.

There is no denying the fact that there is a psychic element to UFOs; and even though Adamski tried to convince his followers that all of his contacts were of a strict physical nature, we cannot turn against the weight of evidence that there might have been some grand-master 'cosmic plan' for him that eventually enabled him to communicate with a Nordic-type ufonaut in the desert" (Beckley, 2009).

On the same matter Colin Bennett offers the following: "Adamski's 'core story' began to run out of steam very quickly...His followers demanded to know more about Orthon the 'spaceman,' and they asked if Adamski had been on yet more journeys in Orthon's flying saucer. Adamski, the all-American showman, anxious not to disappoint, then turned back to literature, as it were, in order to create new episodes for life. This got him into a terrible wrap-round tangle, and subsequently he pasted-up any and every kind of covered-wagon to try and keep the Orthon story going. This lost him almost all of his latter-day following, and he was finished. But history refused to erase him. The core story was archetypal; it had a kind of irresistible intellectual eroticism about it" (Bennett, 2009).

3

The FBI Takes Note

Further illuminating data on Adamski can be gleaned from studying a file that none other than the FBI secretly compiled on him that covered a clearly delineated period almost post-dating the Orthon encounter and that continued for a decade. Given the controversial nature of the secret dossier, Adamski was very lucky that it did not surface publicly within his lifetime. Had it done so, it would surely have left many of his followers wholly disillusioned. Fortunately for Adamski, however, the provisions of the Freedom of Information Act require that all FBI files on specific individuals must remain exempt from public access until after the person at issue has passed away.

The FBI's surveillance of Adamski commenced in 1950, and reveals the illuminating fact that the FBI considered Adamski to be nothing less than an outrageous subversive. An examination of the files reveals that the bulk of the early background data on Adamski and his actions was provided to the FBI by a source whose identity has been carefully deleted from all of the now-publicly-available files. They do reflect, however, that it was on September 5, 1950—at its San Diego office—that the FBI's source elected to reveal all he knew about Adamski:

[Source] advised the San Diego Office that he first met Adamski about three months ago at the café which is named the Palomar Gardens Café, owned and operated by Adamski, at the road junction, five miles East of Rincon, California, at a point where the highway branches off leading to Mount Palomar Observatory. [Source] became involved in a lengthy conversation with Adamski during which Adamski told them at great length of his findings of flying saucers and so forth. He told them of a spaceship which he said he saw between the Earth and the moon, which he estimated to be approximately three miles in length, which was flying so fast that he had to take about 80 photographs before he could get three of them to turn out.

According to [Source] Adamski stated that the Federal Communications Commission, under the direction of the 'Military Government' of the United States, has established communication with the people from other worlds, and has learned that they are so much more advanced than the inhabitants of this earth that they have deciphered the languages used here. Adamski stated that in this interplanetary communication, the Federal Communications Commission asked the inhabitants of the other planet concerning the type of government they had there and the reply indicated that it was very different from the democracy of the United States. Adamski stated that his answer was kept secret by the United States Government, but he added, 'If you ask me they probably have a Communist form of government and our American government wouldn't release that kind of thing, naturally. That is a thing of the future—more advanced' (FBI, 1950).

One does not have to be a genius to realize that Adamski's assertions that his long-haired alien friends were nothing less than full-on Russia-loving Reds led the FBI to elevate its secret spying on the man to a whole new level. And, as the files show, it was the following that led J. Edgar Hoover to conclude that Adamski's actions should be classified as a "security matter." The files state:

Adamski, during this conversation, made the prediction that Russia will dominate the world and we will then have an era of peace for 1,000 years. He stated that Russia already has the atom bomb and the hydrogen bomb and that the great earthquake, which was reported behind the Iron Curtain recently, was actually a hydrogen bomb explosion being tried out by the Russians. Adamski states this 'earthquake' broke seismograph machines and he added that no normal earthquake can do that.

Adamski stated that within the next 12 months, San Diego will be bombed. Adamski stated that it does not make any difference if the United States has more atom bombs than Russia inasmuch as Russia needs only 10 atom bombs to cripple the United States by placing these simultaneously on such spots as Chicago and other vital centers of this country. The United States today is in the same state of deterioration as was the Roman Empire prior to its collapse and it will fall just as the Roman Empire did. The Government in this country is a corrupt form of government and capitalists are enslaving the poor (FBI, 1950).

The FBI was not impressed at all.

Things got worse for Adamski in January 1953 when the FBI was told that "Adamski had in his possession a machine which could draw 'flying saucers' and airplanes down from the sky" (FBI, 1953).

One can only imagine the consternation running throughout the corridors of power when this bit of gossip surfaced: not only was Adamski a devotee of Commie-aliens; he was now a potential threat to the airline industry, too. Or was he?

Although Adamski championed the idea that "Russia will dominate the world and we will then have an era of peace for 1,000 years" (FBI, 1950), he did express some concern that this aircraft-destroying machine might be used against American airplanes. As a result of wanting to make his position clear, Adamski decided to contact U.S. authorities to reveal the truth. As a result, agents of both the FBI and the Air Force's Office of Special Investigations met with Adamski on January 12, 1953. A worried Adamski tried to explain to the grim-faced agents that the device was actually the brainchild of someone else; and despite what the FBI might have heard to the contrary, Adamski had not had the opportunity to view the aircraft-destroying machine. But, in an effort to try and look patriotic and appease the FBI, Adamski admitted that he had enough awareness of the machine's creator to tactfully describe him as being not "entirely loyal"

(FBI, 1953). On this matter at least, Adamski did cooperate with the Air Force and the FBI.

In that same meeting, Adamski felt compelled to inform the agents of his encounter with Orthon. Whether this was merely the result of his ego, or a desire to advise the agents of the alleged alien presence on Earth, is unknown. But the FBI did not ignore what he had to say and prepared the following:

> At a point 10 2/10 miles from Desert Center on the road to Parker and Needles, Arizona, [Adamski] made contact with a space craft and had talked to a space man. Adamski stated that he, [deleted] and his wife Mary had been out in the desert and that he and the persons with him had seen the craft come down to the earth. Adamski stated that a small stairway in the bottom of the craft, which appeared to be a round disc, opened and a space man came down the steps. Adamski stated he believed there were other space men in the ship because the ship appeared translucent and could see the shadows of the space men (FBI, 1953).

Adamski continued to divulge details to the FBI, adding that the alien was "over five feet in height, having long hair like a woman's and garbed in a suit similar to the space suits or web suits worn by the U.S. Air Force men" (FBI, 1953). He also advised the unsmiling officials that the sole means of communication was sign language, and that he was firmly of the opinion that his mind was being read. In support of this assertion, Adamski told the G-Men the much-repeated story of how, as he prepared to take a picture of the flying saucer, Orthon motioned him to halt. Adamski continued that he ignored the warning, after which Orthon wrestled the camera out of Adamski's hands and headed off into the sky. In other words, whether we take Adamski's words as gospel or not, behind closed doors he was telling the same story as that which he was relating to the world at large. The FBI recorded yet further data demonstrating that Adamski's tales of alien contact never really wavered to any significant degree:

> Adamski further advised that he had obtained plaster casts of the footprints of the space man and stated that the casts indicated the footprints had designs on them similar to the signs of the Zodiac. On January 12, 1953, Adamski advised that on December 13, 1952, the space ship returned to the Palomar Gardens and

came low enough to drop the [film negative] which the space man had taken from him, Adamski, and had then gone off over the hill. Adamski stated that when he had the negatives developed at a photo shop in Escondido, California, that the negative that the space man had taken from him contained writing which he believed to be the writing of the space men. Adamski furnished the writer with copies of the space writing and photographs of the space ship (FBI, 1953).

Interestingly, the FBI was informed by another individual that: "The photographs were taken by setting the camera lens at infinity, which would sharpen the background of mountains and trees and blurs the saucer, which was probably strung on a thin wire. [Source] advised that if the camera were set at infinity the wire would not show" (FBI, 1953).

From March 1953 onward, the FBI's dealings with Adamski became more serious and revolved around what was said by the man during a lecture for the Californian Lions Club two weeks previously. FBI documentation revealed Adamski had prefaced his controversial lecture with the revelation that "his material had all been cleared with the Federal Bureau of Investigation and Air Force Intelligence" (FBI, 1953). It must be stressed that this particularly notable episode raised major red flags about Adamski and his credibility.

Again, agents of both the FBI and the Air Force paid a visit to Adamski and "severely admonished him" for implying that his claims had their endorsement (FBI, 1953). Both the FBI and the Air Force demanded Adamski sign a document admitting that his statements most assuredly did not have any form of governmental or military blessing. With one copy of the statement retained by Adamski, extra copies were placed on-file with FBI agents in Dallas, Texas; Los Angeles, California; and Cleveland, Ohio, due to the fact that "these offices have received previous communications concerning [Adamski]" (FBI, 1953).

Nearly a year later, Adamski again found himself in deep trouble of the official kind: A representative of the Los Angeles–based Better Business Bureau turned up one morning at the Los Angeles FBI office and informed the bemused agents that the BBB was investigating Adamski's 1953 book, *Flying Saucers Have Landed*, to determine if it was nothing less than an outrageous hoax on the general public. The BBB further informed the

Los Angeles office that, as part of its attempt to unravel fact from fiction, Adamski had been interviewed by a BBB staff member—an interview that was highly notable for the following, specific reason: During the interview, Adamski gave the BBB interviewer a tantalizing glimpse of a piece of paper that had "a blue seal in the lower left corner, at the top of which appeared the names of three Government agents"—one from the FBI and two from the Air Force (FBI, 1953). The implication was that the FBI and the Air Force were endorsing Adamski's claims—and, by default, his book with Desmond Leslie, *Flying Saucers Have Landed.*

The document was an audacious hoax. Investigations undertaken by a Special Agent Willis of the San Diego FBI revealed that the "document" was nothing less than an altered version of the statement that the FBI and the Air Force had made him sign nearly a year earlier. Not content with claiming to have met aliens, Adamski was apparently now in the business of forging government documents, too!

An FBI memorandum of December 16, 1953, written by the head of the FBI's public relations department, Louis B. Nicholls, detailed the sorry saga:

[Deleted] instructed Willis to call on Adamski at the Palomar Gardens Café, Valley Center, California. This is located five miles east of Rincon, California, near the Mount Palomar Observatory. Willis was told to have the San Diego agents, accompanied by representatives of OSI if they care to go along, call on Adamski and read the riot act in no uncertain terms pointing out he has used this document in a fraudulent, improper manner, that this Bureau has not endorsed, approved, or cleared his speeches or book, that he knows it, and the Bureau will simply not tolerate any further foolishness, misrepresentations, and falsity on his part. Willis was told to instruct the Agents to diplomatically retrieve, if possible, the document in issue from Adamski. Willis said he would do this and send in a report at once (FBI, 1953).

Although plans to prosecute Adamski were discussed by the FBI, no action was ever taken: Officialdom astutely realized that any attempts to punish Adamski would likely be perceived by UFO researchers as evidence that Adamski was on the right track in terms of his alien pursuits; and that, as a result, the Government was doing all it could to prevent him

The deserts of California—home to numerous alien encounters. Photo courtesy of Nick Redfern.

from revealing the cosmic truth. So, the FBI merely seethed—peeved that Adamski had escaped with barely a warning. But the FBI-Adamski relationship was not over.

In 1957, a good-natured hoax was perpetrated on Adamski by Jim Moseley—a long-time observer of the UFO scene and the editor of the newsletter, *Saucer Smear*—and Gray Barker, author of the book *They Knew Too Much About Flying Saucers*. Moseley states: "Gray Barker had a friend who is still alive now and begged me never to reveal his name, but at the time was a kid of 18 or 20 years of age, whose father was rather high in the State Department. He wandered into his father's office and stole some official State Department stationery, about six or seven different kinds" (Bishop, 1995).

Some of that same stationery wound up in the hands of Moseley and Barker, at which point the pair decided to create what has become known within the realm of UFO research as the "Straith Letter," as Moseley explains:

So, one night Barker and I got together at his place in Clarksburg, West Virginia and wrote six or seven different letters to people in the field. And the Straith letter was so-called because it was signed by R.E. Straith of the 'Cultural Affairs Committee' of the State Department, and we deliberately made that part up because it didn't exist. There was a committee with a similar name, but Straith did not exist.

We opened the letter: 'Dear Professor Adamski,' which was flattering him because he wasn't a professor at all; he just made that up. And it said in essence that 'there are some of us here that know of your contacts and we are behind you all the way, but we cannot come out publicly to support you at this time. But rest assured that we are behind you in spirit,' and so on. That was the gist of the letter; and whether Adamski thought it was a hoax or not didn't really matter, since it was just what he wanted to hear.

So, [Adamski] publicized it; and after a few months the FBI came to him and told him to stop it. They told him it was a hoax and to stop saying that it was genuine. This was just what he needed, and he started crowing that the FBI had harassed him, and so that meant it had to be genuine. There were then two investigations by the FBI and the State Department. They went down and talked to Barker, since someone noticed that the typing on this letter was just like the ones he sent to all kinds of people. Barker got very paranoid after this and took the typewriter and broke it into many little pieces. Then he found where they were building a wall somewhere in Clarksburg [West Virginia], and dumped the pieces in. So, to this day that typewriter is buried in a wall somewhere in that town (Ibid.)

It was just another surreal aspect of the on-going saga of George Adamski vs. the FBI.

In early 1959, Adamski delivered a series of lectures in New Zealand. Notably, this lecture-tour was of interest to the world of officialdom, and his presentations were clandestinely scrutinized by government operatives.

A Foreign Service Dispatch of February 1959 was sent from the American Embassy in New Zealand to the FBI and summarized Adamski's activities in New Zealand. It read:

Mr. George ADAMSKI, the Californian 'flying saucer expert' and author of the book *The Flying Saucers Have Landed* and others, has been visiting New Zealand for the last two weeks. He has given well-attended public lectures in Auckland and Wellington as well as meetings with smaller groups of 'saucer' enthusiasts. In Wellington his lecture filled the 2,200 seats in the Town Hall. He was not permitted to charge for admission as the meeting was held on a Sunday night, but a 'silver coin' collection was taken up and this would more than recoup his expenses.

Adamski's lectures appear to cover the usual mass of sighting reports, pseudo-scientific arguments in support of his theories and his previously well-publicized 'contacts' with saucers and men from Venus. He is repeating his contention that men from other planets are living anonymously on the earth and, according to the press, said in Auckland that there may be as many as 40,000,000 of these in total. He is also making references to security restrictions and saying that the U.S. authorities know a lot more than they will tell.

The report of Adamski's lecture in Wellington in *The Dominion* was flanked by an article by Dr. I.L. THOMPSON, Director of the Carter Observatory, vigorously refuting Adamski on a number of scientific points. However, the news report of the lecture called it 'the best Sunday night's entertainment Wellington has seen for quite a time.' Interest in flying saucers in New Zealand seems to be roughly comparable to that in the United States. There is a small but active organization which enthusiasts have supported for some years. This organization publishes a small paper and receives and circulates stories of sightings. At the Adamski lecture in Wellington, approximately 40 members of the 'Adamski Corresponding Society' wore blue ribbons and sat in reserved seats in the front row. Press reports suggest that Adamski probably is making no new converts to saucer credence in his current tour. His audiences have given forth with a certain amount of 'incredulous murmuring' and are said to be totally unimpressed with his pictures of saucers (FBI, 1959).

Almost 12 months later, Adamski was again the topic of FBI interest when an unidentified American citizen offered an opinion that Adamski was using the UFO controversy as a means to promote communism. The FBI recorded the following:

> [Censored] said that in recent weeks she and her husband had begun to wonder if Adamski is subtly spreading Russian propaganda. She said that, according to Adamski, the 'space people' are much better people than those on Earth; that they have told him the Earth is in extreme danger from nuclear tests and that they must be stopped; that they have found peace under a system in which churches, schools, individual governments, money, and private property were abolished in favor of a central governing council, and nationalism and patriotism have been done away with; that the 'space people' want nuclear tests stopped immediately and that never should people on earth fight; if attacked, they should lay down their arms and welcome their attackers.

> [Censored] said the particular thing that first made her and her husband wonder about Adamski was a letter they received from him dated 10/12/59, in which it was hinted that the Russians receive help in their outer space programs from the 'space people,' and that the 'space people' will not help any nation unless such nation has peaceful intent. It occurred to them that the desires and recommendations of the 'space people' whom Adamski quotes are quite similar to Russia's approach, particularly as to the ending of nuclear testing, and it was for this reason she decided to call the FBI (FBI, 1960).

From then on, the worlds of the FBI and Adamski never again crossed paths. Colin Bennett states with respect to Adamski's fraught relationship with the FBI:

> Back in 1952, the FBI regarded Adamski as little more than a pop-eyed hippy nutcase. He was, however, beginning to get a certain following, and he was watched as much later, John Lennon, Timothy Leary, Andrija Puharich, and Wilhelm Reich were watched. We can assume all possible cult followers, right up to the present day are taken note of in a similar manner. The flying saucer bit probably did not interest the FBI at all, even if they knew, cared, or understood anything about such things.

On the other hand, they might well have been interested in Adamski's racial and near-Nazi views. He did not make a big thing of such opinions, but he certainly voiced them after the War, at a time when hundreds of thousands of dead Americans were fresh in the memory, and that could not have gone down well. Another level of Intelligence interest might have been aroused concerning possible observation of unusual airborne devices which might well have been advanced, secret surveillance craft of some kind, possibly launched from Russian submarines off the West Coast. There was also another good reason for suspicion. In the 1950s, myriad tests were being carried out on jets, rockets, and missiles in the Mojave Desert where Orthon appeared originally. Many of these tests were carried out by imported Nazis rocket-scientists and technological experts, secretly smuggled into the U.S. by means of Operation Paperclip. Intelligence surveillance in this area was therefore high, for by 1953, the race for the Moon had just commenced. Reports of exotic airborne vehicles may well have leaked from the Mojave area and created all kinds of 'alien craft' rumors.

Yet another reason for surveillance of Adamski was that security agencies of any and every kind operate on the principle that cults can turn political very quickly, and often in a very nasty way. As we know, countless assassins and terrorists arise from cults of many kinds. Official interest, to my mind, was therefore a passing criminal interest, not an esoteric one; although Adamski in his semi-paranoid act as a rather comical anarchist tried to make it so, implying all kinds of motivations to even minimal gumshoe levels of official enquiry. It must be remembered that before he became a famous author with a best-selling book, he was the kind of guy who sounded off about anything and everything. His murky 'occult' involvements with the esoteric underground on the wild West Coast between the time of his youth in World War 1 and the 1950s marked him out as a very odd character indeed (Bennett, 2009).

Bennett adds with respect to Adamski:

"I asked myself: why should we be so alarmed by a man who says he met a supposed extraterrestrial being who stepped out of a so-called flying saucer? Why should such a man be regarded as a threat and be ridiculed for his trouble? It appears that certain kinds of fantastic claim, no matter how apparently ridiculous and plain stupid, somehow get to the core of our belief system, and momentarily push aside all plain practical rationalizations and thoroughly disturb our iron-bound consciousness. Most structured, factual arguments just do not have this kind of power. It appears that all things out of the ordinary are mental dynamite. They must be carefully managed by whatever control system is operational at any one time, whether religious, scientific, or military. The original Adamski 'contact' story makes us stare into an abyss, and our psychological management system tries automatically to shut this down; if only to allow us to get some sleep at night" (Ibid).

The final word on Adamski, for now at least, goes to Jim Moseley:

In 1953, I got interested in saucers and met a professional writer who basically said: 'If you go around the country and do all the work, and interview these people who have made various claims about seeing saucers and meeting aliens, then I'll put it together and we'll co-author a flying saucer book.' So, I did that; but the book never happened, until I used my notes in my own book, forty-nine-years later. But, in '53, I had time and money; so I took my car around the country for several weeks: from New York, by a southern route, to California. Then I came back through the middle of the country. I interviewed at least 100 people on that trip who had been mentioned in the early saucer books: military people, scientists, and George Adamski.

When I met him, Adamski was in his classic mode of the great guru. You could go to him at Palomar without an appointment and he would be sitting there, holding court, and talking to all the people that came in. He seemed like a pleasant sort. He couldn't prove anything: you had the choice of believing him or not. Now, whether he was genuine or not, he did have a background with the Royal Order of Tibet. Then he wrote his science fiction story, *Pioneers of Space*, which turned out to be very similar to his later UFO book. I don't think he literally believed everything he said. But I think what he said was in-line with a personal philosophy that he may very well have taken seriously.

I think with Adamski it was like this: if I say 'I'm Jim Moseley, and I believe in world-peace, love, and saving the environment,' people won't care. Why should they? But if I say that a spaceman called Orthon told me that we should love each other; well, that certainly gives it more meaning. I think that is one of the big things behind the Contactee movement. They believed in what they were saying; but they needed a higher authority to get it across. Like in religion, you need God. Adamski needed Orthon (Moseley, 2009).

George Adamski, without doubt the ultimate Contactee, died from the effects of a heart attack on April 23, 1965.

4

Close Encounters
With the Captain

Beyond any shadow of doubt, the number of people who can claim aliens wrecked their marriages is infinitely small. But, such claims have been made—the most memorable being that of construction worker Truman Bethurum. His idea of a close encounter was very different from those of other UFO witnesses: his alleged liaisons in the summer of 1952 with Space Captain Aura Rhanes, a supposed citizen of the planet Clarion, ultimately led his outraged wife to file for divorce!

Bethurum was born in 1898 in California. He married and divorced wife number one in the early stages of the Second World War, at which point he gravitated toward factory work. At the close of the War, Bethurum met his second wife, Mary, whom he married in October 1945. But Bethurum soon got restless: "The humdrum was telling on my nerves, and I decided my first choice for a change would be outside construction work, repair and maintenance of equipment" (Bethurum, 1954).

Bethurum didn't know it, but high-strangeness was looming. In June 1952, Bethurum and Mary were living in Santa Barbara, California.

During the last week of that month Bethurum received a phone call from a friend, E.E. "Whitey" Edwards, who offered him a lucrative job working on a new stretch of highway in Clark County, approximately 70 miles from Las Vegas. Although initially reluctant to accept a job that would place him in the heart of the Nevada desert, Bethurum finally relented, and took a position as a maintenance mechanic, working the swing shift from 4 p.m. until the early hours. It wasn't long before Bethurum's other-worldly encounters began in earnest.

Situated not far from the highway is a place called Mormon Mesa, a 1,893-foot high summit that dominates the Moapa Valley. Between the mesa and its two, near-identical neighbors, are two huge chasms created by the Muddy and Virgin rivers that carved the mesa eons ago. Visually stunning, both then and now, Mormon Mesa was about to become a veritable hotbed of alien activity. Bethurum's wife was a collector of seashells; and as the area had been covered by ocean during prehistoric times, after he finished his shift, Bethurum headed out to the Mesa to see if he could find any fossilized shells as a gift for his wife—who had decided not to accompany her husband to Nevada, and instead elected to remain in Santa Barbara. Yes: The cracks in the relationship were already showing.

Bethurum searched the pitch-black area for a couple of hours; but, having failed to find any such seashells, returned to his truck "to take a little snooze" (Bethurum, 1954). It was while snoozing—or while, it might be argued, he was in an altered state-of-mind—that Bethurum was blessed with a visit from the inhabitants of another world: the Clarionites. An hour or so after falling asleep, said Bethurum, he was awakened by what he described as "mumbling" (Bethurum, 1954). As he began to stir, Bethurum was shocked to see that his truck was surrounded by between eight and 10 men. They were all olive-skinned, around 5 feet in height, wearing uniforms and black-billed caps—and who were in stark contrast to the long-haired, hippy-types that hung out with George Adamski.

Then to Bethurum's amazement, he saw sitting on Mormon Mesa, and only a short distance from him, a "great circular monster" (Bethurum, 1954). It was nothing less than a 300-foot diameter honest-to-goodness flying saucer that was about 18 feet deep, and had the appearance of burnished stainless steel. At that point, the little men began enthusiastically crowding around Bethurum—all, somewhat oddly, wanting to shake hands. Then

Bethurum made the fatal mistake that led down the rocky road to divorce. He asked one of the men if they had a captain. They did. As Bethurum later recalled in excited tones: "Little did I suspect that their captain would turn out to be a woman—and what a woman!" (Bethurum, 1954).

After asking his fateful question, something remarkable happened: The group of little beings invited Bethurum aboard their spacecraft. Somewhat amusingly—and perhaps anticipating that Bethurum would find their captain to be definitively hot stuff—one of the aliens warned the startled road-worker "not to try any funny business" (Ibid.).

It's clear from a study of Bethurum's testimony that he was instantly captivated by the space captain. Describing her as "the queen of women," he revealed that her skin "was a beautiful olive and roses," and that she had a "flashing smile" (Ibid.).

But, for all her attractions, she remained steadfastly elusive and enigmatic. When Bethurum asked her where she was from, she replied— in what Bethurum perceived were evasive tones: "Time and distance are of no concern to us, and what you call time and distance is inconsequential in our lives." Further questions followed, as did the stunted replies, on matters pertaining to religion and their technology. Then, finally, the captain announced it was time for them to leave. But, in a fashion that would have made Arnold Schwarzenegger's *Terminator* proud in the extreme, she carefully added: "We'll be back" (Bethurum, 1957).

So Bethurum said, the captain kept her word: Around 3.30 a.m. on either August 3rd or 4th, and after seeing what he described as something like "a meteor falling through the starlit purple night," Bethurum "swerved [his] truck and hit out across the desert," a mile or so from the highway (Ibid.). Sure enough, there was the gigantic saucer, sitting ominously on the dusty floor, looking just like its fictional counterpart from *The Day the Earth Stood Still*. As before, a group of little men was in evidence. Then there was the highlight of the night: The captain of the craft again put in an appearance. On this occasion, she was slightly more talkative and revealed the name of her planet (Clarion), the fact that her race was free of illness, and that the "flowers and animals" of her world were very different to ours (Ibid.). Soon afterward, the captain signified that Bethurum's visit was over. But trouble of a very terrestrial kind was brewing.

Before Bethurum's third encounter with the people of Clarion occurred, he received in the mail a letter from his wife, Mary. Once again—as a result, she said, of Nevada's overpowering summer heat, and the fact that she was looking after her granddaughter—Mary was reluctant to come and spend some time with Bethurum. Perceiving this as an excuse, he wisely decided it might not be a good idea to talk about his nighttime liaisons with an alien space-babe. And those liaisons were only set to increase: The next meeting occurred on August 18; once again high upon Mormon Mesa.

As Bethurum described the events in question, it was around 1:30 a.m., and the giant craft landed no more than about 200 yards from where his truck was parked. Once more, "the little lady again appeared at the opening and beckoned me to come aboard, which I willingly and gladly did." It was then, as Bethurum "eyed her flesh quite a bit" that he finally learned the captain's name: Aura Rhanes (Bethurum, 1970).

As before, the topic of conversation was enigmatic and elusive, and just like the previous occasion, the meeting was over barely a short time after it had begun. "Remember us," Rhanes told Bethurum in almost ethereal fashion, before her craft silently soared into the darkened heavens (Ibid.). Needless to say, Bethurum did remember them. He didn't have long to wait to see them again either. Seven days later, Captain Rhanes and her crew were back.

Bethurum was once more invited aboard the mighty saucer. This time, he learned a little more about the home world of Captain Rhanes: Clarion, a planet "on the other side of the moon" that was invisible to the people of Earth, "due to moisture, clouds and light reflectors making an impenetrable screen" (Ibid.). This, of course, was a classic example of the less-than-scientific—and possibly deliberately deceitful—gobbledygook spouted by so many of the Space-Brothers to those they deemed worthy of contact. Although nothing of a particularly spectacular nature occurred on this occasion, on the following day something most assuredly did.

Around 3:30 a.m., and after finishing his shift, Bethurum met with his boss and friend Whitey at a restaurant in Glendale, where they dined on an early breakfast. While there, said Bethurum, "I bugged my eyes out." Bethurum said that at the restaurant sat a woman "whom I believe to this day was Captain Aura Rhanes," along with one of the crew members that Bethurum recognized from an earlier, clandestine meeting atop Mormon

Mesa. Wearing a black-and-red beret, and dark and large sunglasses, and with the collar of her jacket turned up high, she exhibited what was practically an air of hostility when Bethurum tentatively walked over to the pair's table and asked, "I beg your pardon, lady, but haven't we met before?" (Bethurum, 1958).

"No" was the one-word reply, offered in a decidedly menacing tone. Bethurum persisted, but merely got "another low no" (Ibid.). Sensing that his presence was most definitely not wanted, Bethurum returned to his table—shortly after which the apparent alien pair settled the check and hastily headed for the door, and the pre-dawn darkness. Rather oddly, the waitress told Bethurum she noticed that the man accompanying the presumed Captain Rhanes had a "penciled on" scar on his face (Ibid.).

There was a far stranger aspect to that night's activities: At the same time Bethurum was trying to engage the disguised pair in conversation, Whitey stepped outside for a cigarette. Yet, when Bethurum tried to follow the little man and woman as they exited the door, they seemingly vanished into oblivion. "They never came out," said Whitey. "Honest, Tru, not a blessed soul passed through that door until you came out" (Ibid.).

Following this encounter, Bethurum decided it was finally time to come clean with his wife. He related the whole story: the initial landing on Mormon Mesa of the gigantic flying saucer, the appearance of the little men, and his somewhat intimate chats with Captain Aura Rhanes. Mary was neither impressed nor sympathetic. She had no time for flying saucers, no time for aliens, and certainly no time for the delicious space captain. In other words, it seemed highly unlikely that an intergalactic three-way was on the cards. Instead, according to Bethurum, following receipt of the letter, Mary expressed major concerns about his health and sanity, and made it clear to Bethurum that traveling to Nevada to meet with a group of dwarfish extraterrestrials was hardly a priority for her. Bethurum got the message: As on each and every previous occasion, Bethurum's subsequent close encounters were of the definitively solitary kind. According to Bethurum, the fifth visit from the aliens occurred on the night of September 5th, just a short distance from Mormon Mesa.

By all accounts, this was a relatively unspectacular meeting: Bethurum woefully told Captain Rhanes that "my wife thinks I've gone off my rocker," while Rhanes alluded to the possibility that perhaps Bethurum might one day take a flight into space with her (Ibid.). That, of course, perked him up big time. Somewhat outrageously, Bethurum claimed that the next time he saw Aura Rhanes was on September 6th, while getting his hair cut in downtown Las Vegas! In a situation that paralleled his experience at the diner, Bethurum tried to speak with Rhanes: He raced out of the barber's shop as he saw her strolling past the window, and shouted, "Lady, lady!" Once again, not wishing to engage in conversation, she merely shook her head in Bethurum's direction, and quickly melted into the crowd. But, as Rhanes had earlier promised, she would be back.

Acting on impulse, later that same night Bethurum headed out to "a desert spot near Henderson," where the aliens landed, and told Bethurum, "Our captain wishes to see you" (Bethurum, 1970).

"We talked of many things, of the earth, stars, planets and moon, and of the time I will go along for a visit to Clarion," said Bethurum (Ibid.). Then he made the unfathomable mistake of telling Mary of his latest adventures of the Aura kind. Pleased, she was not.

Mary accused Bethurum of trying to make her jealous, with all the talk of the beautiful Captain Rhanes. But she was having none of it: "It won't work. I'm not jealous. And I'm not coming up there in all that heat" (Ibid.). Take that, Truman.

Bethurum was hardly moved by Mary's hostile response: by this time, he was overwhelmingly taken with Aura Rhanes. On September 16, in yet another late-night encounter, Bethurum asked the captain if he could take a trip to Clarion and see her world. That was fine—providing he didn't bring Mary along. "I don't think that would be advisable," said Rhanes, icily (Bethurum, 1958). The green-eyed monster, it seems, was as well known on Clarion as it was on Earth.

The conversation continued, and Bethurum was led to believe that a trip to the alien world was very possibly on the cards, and he exited the craft full of anticipation for the incredible journey that might well be looming. By now, Bethurum was incapable of getting the cosmic captain off of his mind: "Tops in shapeliness and beauty" was how he described her after this particular encounter. Then, while on the Clarionites' craft on the night of October 2, 1952, all that a salivating Bethurum could think about was how Captain Rhanes's "fully developed small figure" was "set off" by her slacks, "which appeared almost as if painted on her, so snugly did they fit" (Bethurum, 1954). He certainly had a way with words—if not with his wives.

Two more encounters followed—the tenth on October 12th, when the possibility of Bethurum taking a trip to Clarion was again discussed, and during which Rhanes playfully teased Bethurum by telling him that "our climate is mild enough for you to sleep in the nude if you wish," and that "you will find our beds are the finest to relax body and mind" (Bethurum, 1995). Ahem.

As the meeting drew to a close, Rhanes told Bethurum that "if all conditions are right," she and her crew would meet him very soon for a trip to their world (Ibid.). Sadly for Bethurum it was not to be. Instead, on the next night, the Clarionites dropped a small flare near an old power line that skirted the hills northeast of Glendale. The flare was easily located by Bethurum, who said that nearby was a foot-square package that had a four-word note inscribed on its outside: *To Truman From Aura*. It contained two additional flares that Bethurum was to use if he wished to contact the Clarionites again.

It was useful, indeed, that Bethurum had been provided the flares; since he shortly thereafter changed his employment: He took a new job as a welder on Nevada's Davis Dam. This was of no particular matter, however, as the Clarionites were fully aware of Bethurum's every move. On the night of November 2nd, anxious to see Captain Rhanes again, he fired one of the flares in a remote, desert area not too far from Kingman, Arizona. Rhanes and her crew were quickly on the scene. For the final time, Bethurum was invited aboard the saucer and the pair chatted at length about life on their respective worlds, their hobbies, and much more of a friendly nature.

At the end of the exchange, there was no real indication that this was to be their last meeting—and yet, it certainly was. Rhanes escorted Bethurum out of the saucer and back to the desert floor, where they bid each other farewell. In a few moments, Bethurum was alone, standing in the stark desert darkness, watching in awe as the huge alien craft grew ever smaller as it rose silently into the starlit sky.

Perhaps wisely, at that point Bethurum's thoughts returned to Mary. He begged her to come and visit him, and finally she relented: just before Christmas, 1952. But the damage was done: Mary told Bethurum she could not believe any part of his wild story, intimated that he had most likely fabricated everything, and said she had no wish to head out to the desert with him after sunset, in search of aliens that were "tops in shapeliness and beauty" or otherwise. She quickly returned to California, leaving a crushed Bethurum utterly alone in the barren desert.

Then it occurred to him: he had the remaining flare. Excitedly, late one night, as February 1953 drew to a close, Bethurum again headed for the desert, and fired the flare high into the sky. However, a forlorn Bethurum reported that: "…the hours passed and dawn came up over the eastern horizon, with no sign at all to tell me that my signal had been observed" (Bethurum, 1995).

"Disconsolate and disappointed," Bethurum headed home—to Mary— in hopes of saving his strained marriage (Ibid.). For a while it seemed to go okay. Mary warned Bethurum that if things were to work she did not wish to hear any more talk of "little men and beautiful space captains," and the pair tried valiantly to make things work (Ibid.). But it was all too little, and far too late. The pair eventually divorced—Mary unable to compete with the alluring specter of Captain Aura Rhanes that was ever-present. But, despite divorce, things were on the up for Bethurum.

In September 1953 the *Redondo Beach Daily Breeze* published an article on his claimed encounters. Then, in 1954, he wrote a book on the subject: *Aboard a Flying Saucer*—after which he quit his job and set himself up as the spiritual leader of the Sanctuary of Thought: a commune he established near Prescott, Arizona. More books followed: *The Voice of Clarion*; *Facing Reality*; and his final book, *The People of the Planet Clarion* (which was published posthumously, in 1970). Interestingly, and highly significantly, an after-word to *The People of the Planet Clarion* written by artist Columba Krebs (who had assisted Bethurum on three of his titles) stated that Bethurum was clearly obsessed by Rhanes, and had even hired a secretary who closely resembled the space captain. But none of this obsession prevented Bethurum from marrying for a third time, in 1961, to a woman named Alvira Roberts. Precisely what Aura Rhanes thought of the wedding, we do not know. She never again returned to bedazzle

Bethurum, who passed away on May 21, 1969, entranced to the absolute very end by his chick from another world.

5

Orfeo and the Aliens

In precisely the same time frame that Truman Bethurum was having flirty, nighttime meetings with curvy Captain Aura Rhanes on Mormon Mesa, Nevada, a Californian resident named Orfeo Angelucci was also falling under the spell of the Space-Brothers and Space-Sisters. In many ways, Angelucci's story is as strange, as subjective and as ethereal as that of Bethurum: it is one filled with tales of clandestine late-night liaisons with aliens in remote locales, dream-like encounters of the highly unusual kind, altered states of consciousness and much, much more.

Born Orville Angelucci in 1912, the man had a strange childhood. He was hardly the healthiest of kids, and was diagnosed with "constitutional inadequacy," which led to severe malnutrition, a lack of appetite, and extreme fatigue. Unable to continue his education as a result of his medical condition, a decision was taken to have Angelucci schooled at home—during which period he was finally able to gain some much-needed weight, and began to take the tentative steps upon the rocky road to recovery.

Then, on completing his education, Angelucci began working for his uncle's flooring company in Trenton, New Jersey. During this time two things happened: Angelucci began to develop a deep interest in scientific subjects, and he met an attractive Italian girl named Mabel Borgianni, who was a direct descendent of the infamous Borgia family of Valencia. They soon married, and a year or so later, their first son, Raymond, was born.

Then disaster struck: Angelucci's fragile health got worse and his weight plummeted to an alarming 103 pounds. In his own words: "I suffered a complete physical breakdown" (Angelucci, 2008). Angelucci's doctors were concerned he would not survive the trauma his body was going through; however, he proved them wrong and pulled himself back from the brink. "It was like being reborn," he astutely commented (Ibid.). Maybe it was: From then on, Angelucci's life followed a pathway that took him far away from the world of selling flooring and carpets. His interest in science became an obsession. In the wake of his recovery, Angelucci developed a fascination with electricity and "electromagnetic phenomena," which was somewhat ironic because, in his own words, "…from earliest childhood I had an acute fear or phobia about lightning. During an electrical storm I suffered not only actual bodily pain, but mental perturbation and distress" (Ibid.).

As a result of this escalating interest in science, said Angelucci, it was an ambitious experiment he undertook in the mid-1940s that first exposed him to the twilight world of the Space-Brothers. The date was August 4, 1946, and Angelucci had become concerned by the way in which living things might be affected by exposure to the Earth's upper-atmosphere. As a result, Angelucci had a brainwave: He would launch a balloon high into the sky, with various cultures of the mold aspergillus aboard. And, this is precisely what Angelucci did. On the day at issue, and with almost torturous precision, he carefully placed mold cultures into a variety of little baskets, attaching them to no less than 18 "Navy-type balloons."

Angelucci's family was there to see the odd spectacle, as were a number of his friends, and a reporter from the local *Trentonian* newspaper. Unfortunately, disaster struck: The balloons broke away from their mooring before they could be correctly launched, and promptly soared into the clear, blue sky. But, then, something very weird occurred.

As a distraught Angelucci watched his experiment go catastrophically awry, his father-in-law, Alfred Borgianni, cried out: "Look! There's an airplane, Orfeo. Maybe it will follow your balloons" (Angelucci, 1955). But it was no airplane. As the vehicle came closer into view, everyone could see that it was a large, saucer-shaped device that glistened in the sunshine, and that appeared to follow the balloons; until all of them finally disappeared from sight. Angelucci mused upon the odd event for a few days, but then promptly forgot about it. That is, until the early summer of 1952.

In November 1947, Angelucci, Mabel, Raymond, and his second son, Richard, took an extended trip to Los Angeles. You may not be surprised to learn that this was prompted by yet another bout of bad health for Angelucci, in which weight loss and fatigue were again dominating factors. The family loved the area and decided to stay. Initially, life was a struggle. Angelucci went into business with his father—which, after three years ended in abject failure. He then got a job as the manager of the Los Feliz Club House, and even wrote a screenplay about a trip to the Moon. Hollywood, unfortunately, failed to sit up and take serious notice. Things finally turned around for Angelucci on April 2, 1952, when he secured employment in the Plastics Unit of the Lockheed Aircraft Corporation at Burbank, California—shortly after which, the aliens decided to pay him a visit. Notably, fellow Contactee George Van Tassel was also employed for a time at this very same Lockheed plant.

"Friday, May 23, 1952, was an ordinary day in Burbank, California, insofar as I was concerned," said Angelucci (Angelucci, 1955). It wasn't destined to stay like that. As the day progressed, Angelucci began to feel ill. His nerves were on edge; he began to suffer from heart palpitations; and his hands and arms were affected by "an odd pricking sensation" (Ibid.). Collectively, this sounds like a description of hyperventilation—an anxiety-based condition that causes alarming physical symptoms brought on by breathing too fast and deep. Something ominous was afoot.

Angelucci struggled to cope with the unsettling symptoms until 12:30 a.m., at which point his shift was finally over and he began the drive home. What a bizarre drive it was. Angelucci's eyes glazed over, and the sounds of traffic became "oddly muffled," as he struggled to concentrate on getting home (Angelucci, 1955). It was not to be. As he drove down Victory Boulevard, Angelucci was shocked to see, slightly above his line of vision, a red, glowing, oval-shaped object that was "about five times as large as the red portion of a traffic light" (Ibid.). It seemed to carefully maintain its distance from Angelucci's car, as if beckoning him to follow—which he did. He drove across a bridge spanning the Los Angeles River, and looked on, mesmerized, as the object came to a halt, hovering over the intersection at a "lonely, deserted stretch of road called Forest Lawn Drive" (Ibid.).

On getting closer, Angelucci's hyperventilation worsened, at which point the unidentified visitor began to move again: slowly, and at a low level, down Forest Lawn Drive. After a mile, the object swerved to the right and hung silently and motionless over a small field situated below the level of the road. Angelucci drove his car just about as close as was possible, and stared in awe at the amazing spectacle. Without warning, the red-colored ball shot away at high speed—but not before two smaller, fluorescent green objects, about 3-feet in diameter, flew out of it and headed directly for Angelucci. They hung, magically, only a few feet above his car for a few minutes, after which something dramatic occurred.

Emanating from between the two green balls, said Angelucci, was the sound of a male voice that spoke perfect English. Stressing that he should not be afraid, the voice explained to a shocked Angelucci that he was in direct communication with "friends from another world." The voice asked, "Do you remember your 18 balloons and the mold cultures that you lost in the skies back in New Jersey, Orfeo? Do you also remember the strange, wingless craft that appeared to be observing your activities?" He certainly did (Angelucci, 1955).

The voice then took on reassuring tones: "We were observing your efforts that day as we have watched you since then." It added: "Drink from the crystal cup you will find on the fender of your car, Orfeo." Sure enough, there was indeed a shining goblet on the fender. Suddenly finding himself "very thirsty," Angelucci drained the cup, at which point, he recalled, "… the area between [the two balls of light] began to glow with a soft green light which gradually formed into a luminous three-dimensional screen as the disks themselves faded perceptively" (Angelucci, 2008).

Shockingly, within the screen, Angelucci could see the heads and shoulders of a man and woman whom he described as being "the ultimate of perfection." Their faces took on wide smiles as they began to engage Angelucci in telepathic conversation and as "new comprehensions that would have required hours of conversation to transmit" saturated Angelucci's brain (Ibid.).

With Angelucci's mind elevated, the entity said: "We'll contact you again, Orfeo. But for now, friend, it is goodnight" (Ibid.). The screen vanished, and the two green balls of light disappeared at high speed into the darkened skies above, leaving Angelucci standing alone by his car. The experience was over. But, further developments of the alien kind were only months away.

Angelucci's next alien encounter was on July 23, 1952. Once again, the location of Angelucci's experience was a bridge: the Hyperion Avenue Freeway Bridge, described by Angelucci as casting "dense, oblique shadows down below making it a shadowed no-man's land." Angelucci decided to walk home across a series of vacant lots that were enveloped by the "deep shadows of the bridge." As before, he suddenly felt ill ("with it came the dulling of consciousness" that dominated the first encounter), his arms and legs began to tingle (sure signs of another attack of hyperventilation), and out of the darkness appeared an object that resembled a "huge, misty soap bubble squatting on the ground [and] emitting a fuzzy, pale glow" (Angelucci, 1959).

At first looking wholly intangible, according to Angelucci the form seemed to gain substance and eerily beckoned him forward. Angelucci, acting on gut-instinct alone, apprehensively approached the opening, entered it, and found himself within a large circular room that contained a reclining chair, in which he felt compelled to sit.

For a moment, panic set in: The room darkened, and Angelucci briefly felt an unknown force push against his body. He realized, with a mixture of excitement and fear, that he was on board a craft that was now high in the skies over Los Angeles. It didn't stop there. As he gripped the arms of the chair, Angelucci was amazed by the sight of a window-like opening that suddenly manifested in the wall in front of him: "I trembled as I realized I was actually looking upon a planet from somewhere out in space" (Ibid.).

A familiar alien voice said: "Orfeo, you are looking upon Earth—your home! From here, over a thousand miles away, in space, it appears as the most beautiful planet in the heavens and a haven of peace and tranquility. But you and your Earthly brothers know the true conditions there." The voice offered warnings about the volatile nature of humankind, of the perils that the future would bring if man did not change his violent ways, and of the way in which "the hour of crisis" was fast approaching" (Ibid.).

At that point, the worlds of advanced alien technology and old-time religion seemed to effortlessly melt into one: Angelucci said he heard the Lord's Prayer "played as though by thousands of violins." Meanwhile, the voice cried out: "Beloved friend of Earth, we baptize you now in the true light of the worlds eternal," and the ship was suddenly filled with near-blinding white light (Angelucci, 2008). Semi-conscious by this point, Angelucci once again felt a heavy presence on his body, and realized he was again feeling the effects of the Earth's gravity: He was clearly being taken back home.

As the craft returned to its original point near the Hyperion Avenue Freeway Bridge, Angelucci thought he had "passed through death and attained infinite life." Realizing he was back on the ground, Angelucci stood up and noticed a "strange, shining bit of metal" on the floor of the vehicle. He picked it up, exited through the same door that he had entered through earlier that night, and headed off into the darkness and the comfort of home. Strangely, he said, between leaving the craft and arriving home, the small piece of metal "quivered," "diminished in size," and finally "dissipated into nothingness" (Ibid.).

In the same way that Captain Aura Rhanes seemed to have a particular penchant for meeting Truman Bethurum on Mormon Mesa, so Angelucci's cosmic visitors became enamored by the shadowy Hyperion Avenue Freeway Bridge: The next meeting occurred only weeks later, on August 2nd. This time, the mysterious voice had a name. Walking slowly out of the darkness, a "well-built man...wearing a kind of uniform, bluish in color, perfectly tailored...but apparently without seams..." approached Angelucci and said, "I know that in your mind you have given me a name—I who have remained nameless to you" (Angelucci, 1955).

Angelucci dubbed the man Neptune.

On this occasion, and while the pair stood in the darkness, a deep exchange occurred—on such subjects as humankind's warlike ways, Neptune's fears for the future of the human race, and tales of an ancient world that allegedly existed in our solar system countless centuries ago; before its people utterly destroyed it, and its pummeled remains became that which, today, we call the Asteroid Belt.

Despite the fact that Neptune warned Angelucci "few will believe or even hear your account of our meeting," he did stress that "at most your story will give only greater faith and inner conviction to the few—but it is an important few!" There was a reason why it was important for Angelucci to at least to try and convince people of the validity of his experiences: A "'Great Accident' is very close," declared Neptune. He elaborated that "the fury of the next war will break when it is least expected; when men are talking of peace. I cannot say more." With that said, Neptune offered his goodbyes, adding, "Later, we shall return, but not to you, beloved friend. You will understand the meaning of these words later on" (Ibid.).

There is another similarity between the experience of Truman Bethurum and that of Angelucci: namely, the reluctance of the alleged alien entities to enter into conversation when seen outside of the confines of their designated areas of contact. Angelucci claimed to have seen Neptune—in a bus terminal—when he was there to meet his wife, Mabel, who had been visiting family back in Trenton. Even though Angelucci felt that Neptune "was expecting me," he noted he received a telepathic message from Neptune "not to approach him." Before the encounter was over, and he and Mabel headed home, Angelucci received a significant message from Neptune: "The last time you saw me, Orfeo, I was in a less objectified projection in your three-dimensional world. The purpose being to give you some idea of our true aspect. But now tonight you see me fully objectified. If you did not know who I am, you could not tell me from one of your fellows. Tonight I am no half-phantom, but can move among men as an Earthman. It is not necessary for you to speak to me; you have gained the understanding. You know now that we can appear and function as human beings" (Angelucci, 2008).

Despite Neptune's reluctance to speak openly, this had no effect upon Angelucci's growing stature within the UFO arena.

As stories pertaining to Angelucci's experiences began to spread, he found himself in hot demand on the lecture circuit. Regular meetings, organized by Max Miller, president of Flying Saucers International, were initiated at the Hollywood Hotel, as was a conference at the same hotel, at which a plethora of speakers took to the stage, including George Adamski and Truman Bethurum. Evidently, the aliens heartily approved of this development: They paid Angelucci several more return visits, all in 1953. During the course of one such visit, Angelucci was told that in the distant past, and in some previous form of existence, he had actually been one of the aliens himself. Angelucci was told that in his earlier alien life he went by the name of Neptune—hence the reason why, subconsciously, the name meant so much to him, and why he had decided to give his mysterious visitor at the bridge that particular title.

Interestingly, one of Angelucci's later encounters—in December 1953—took place while he and his wife were visiting family in Trenton, New Jersey. In other words, it seems the aliens were following Angelucci's every move. On this occasion, the location of the meeting was "a shadowed corner of the yard" on the property of his father-in-law.

"You are indeed a dweller in two worlds now, Orfeo," said the alien that Angelucci had dubbed Neptune (Angelucci, 2008).

Angelucci's encounters were not quite over. In late 1954, he accepted a new job in Twentynine Palms, California. According to Angelucci, one evening midway through December he decided to eat at a pleasant diner that was run by a behemoth-type character dubbed by all who knew him as "Tiny." Angelucci later recalled, as he approached the diner: "I felt a strangeness in the air. There is a cosmic spell over the desert most of the time, but tonight the mystery was less distant and intangible; it was close and pulsating." Angelucci's instincts about feeling "strangeness in the air" were right on target (Angelucci, 1959).

According to Angelucci, "as if under a spell," he was drawn to one particular table where a man was sitting and who motioned Angelucci to take a seat (Ibid.). Introducing himself only as Adam—a name he admitted was an alias—the man explained he was a 37-year-old medical doctor from Seattle who had read Angelucci's first book, *The Secret of the Saucers*. Adam also said he was terminally ill, and his time left on Earth was short in the extreme.

But some form of synchronicity had surely brought the pair together, said Adam: With his life ebbing away, Adam has rented a cabin in the Twentynine Palms area, where he intended to spend his final days, pondering on the meaning of life and death. Curiously, said Angelucci, before Adam embarked at length on his extraordinary story, he pulled out of his pocket an oyster-white pellet, handed it to Angelucci, and motioned him to put it in the glass of water—which he did, seemingly without barely a thought.

Whatever its nature, the pellet had a profound effect on Angelucci: "I… swallowed twice from it. At that instant I entered, with Adam, into a more exalted state and everything around me took on a different semblance" (Ibid.). In simple terms, Angelucci had been drugged, possibly by a drug of a particularly mind-bending nature. Adam then decided to reveal all to Angelucci.

Three nights after arriving in Twentynine Palms, Adam told the brain-bent Angelucci that he had seen something remarkable in the skies above the cabin: "a wayward star;" the appearance of which coincided with the sound of all-encompassing music. Suddenly, the "star" grew brighter, and took on the appearance of "a space ship of some sort spiraling down close to Earth" (Ibid.).

A commanding voice suddenly resonated all around the cabin: "Adam, may I speak with you?" (Ibid.)

Adam explained to Angelucci: "I did not answer by word, but in amazement just nodded my consent. Almost at the same time, the air a few yards in front of me shimmered into a congealing form. It became a dome-shaped craft, sitting there on the sand. A lovely woman stood near it, facing me. Her smile was enough to tell me that it was this ship I had seen gracefully spiraling to earth" (Angelucci, 2008).

The woman, who identified herself as Vega, asked the amazed Adam: "…would you like a trip into the new estate which to you, until now, has existed only as a dream, or hope?" Adam nodded. In a fashion that paralleled so many others who claimed close encounters with human-like aliens in this long-gone era, he followed her aboard for a trip into the darkened depths of the solar-system. Also like most of the Contactees, Adam was fed an absolute barrage of pseudo-scientific nonsense: "The molecules of our craft were tightened a little so that the ionized layer around earth would not cause a glare inside [the ship]," Vega less-than-scientifically told Adam at one point (Angelucci, 2008).

In Adam's case, however, the trip was not to another world: It was to a huge spacecraft, "containing a self-composed world 10 miles in diameter and housing 500,000 people," that was allegedly circling the planet Venus. During the visit, Adam, like Truman Bethurum before him, learned much about the aliens, their home-world, and their culture and their beliefs, before finally waking "back in his rented cabin, to the light of the morning sun." The same situation was repeated on one more occasion; after which Vega and her friends bid Adam a final farewell (Ibid.)

With his story told, Adam then invited and encouraged Angelucci to tell his (Adam's) story to one and all in the form of a book—a task that Angelucci finally agreed to undertake. Then, satisfied that Angelucci would stick to his word, Adam mysteriously vanished into the night.

"I knew I would never see him again," a forlorn Angelucci remarked (Ibid.). He was absolutely right. But the fun and games were not quite over for Angelucci. Several more Contactee-driven publications appeared: *Million Year Prophecy*; *Concrete Evidence*; and *Again we Exist*, after which his time in the alien limelight was largely over. Angelucci died on July 24, 1993, adamant to the end that his tales of cosmic encounters with Neptune, Adam, and their ilk were all utterly real.

6
Rocking With Giants

Born in Jefferson, Ohio, in 1910, George Van Tassel was a legendary character within the formative years of the Contactee movement. He both surfaced and peaked in the 1950s, and came close to eclipsing even George Adamski, in the popularity stakes. Close encounters with long-haired aliens, huge conferences held in the California desert, and a definite gift for spreading the sage-like words of the Space-Brothers, all ensured Van Tassel a deserved place within the world of flying saucers.

Van Tassel became fascinated with aviation at a young age, and, after dropping out of high-school, began working at Cleveland Airport, where he secured his pilot's license. At age 20, he headed for California, and took a job in a garage owned by his uncle Glen. Then fate stepped in and changed everything. During the course of working with his uncle, Van Tassel crossed paths with a man named Frank Critzer—a German immigrant who had retired to the deserts of California due to a chronic case of asthma, and who took to prospecting out in the mines near the town of Landers, a community in San Bernadino County. The resourceful

Critzer had hollowed-out a home for himself beneath a large rock in the area known as Giant Rock and deemed sacred by local, Native American Indians.

Van Tassel was captivated by Critzer's life as a desert prospector and adventurer, and convinced his uncle to loan Critzer $30 so that he could purchase some much-needed mining equipment. In return, Van Tassel was to receive a percentage of any profits that might be generated as a result. But it was not to be. At the height of the Second World War, rumors circulated among the close-knit community of Landers that the lonesome Critzer was nothing less than a full-blown Nazi spy, undoubtedly sent to the United States to undertake some nefarious task on behalf of Adolf Hitler and his cronies. As a result of these never-substantiated allegations, local law-enforcement officers paid Critzer a visit in 1942, with the intention of determining the truth.

Unfortunately, what was intended as an interview quickly mutated into a definitive showdown. Critzer, sensing danger, retreated into his carved-out home beneath Giant Rock; at which point the cops responded by throwing canisters of tear gas into his underground lair. Big mistake: One or more of the canisters had a disastrously close encounter with Critzer's dynamite stash, and the man was blown to smithereens.

In 1947, Van Tassel quit his job (as an aircraft engineer with Lockheed), contacted the Bureau of Land Management—under whose jurisdiction the land in question fell and applied for a lease that would allow him to run the then-abandoned airstrip that was adjacent to Giant Rock. The BLM approved everything: Van Tassel soon had a new abode: Critzer's *Flintstones*-style underground house. He was soon hard at work, redeveloping the airstrip, and constructing both a café (called the Come on Inn) and a dude-ranch on the property.

So the legend goes, on moving into the cave, the Van Tassels' were shocked to see the walls still stained red with Critzer's blood. Adding even more to the legend of Van Tassel are the recollections of his half-sister, Margaret Manyo, who says that none other than Howard Hughes (with whom Van Tassel had worked at Lockheed) used to fly in on weekends to indulge in the tasty pies that Mrs. Van Tassel regularly cooked. All was normal for several years—or, at least, as normal as things could ever be for a family that owned a blood-soaked cave under a huge rock and who dined on pie with brilliant fruitcake Howard Hughes. But that all changed late one night in 1951 when the aliens decided it was time to get chummy with Van Tassel.

By Van Tassel's own admission, on the night at issue he was sprawled out on the desert floor ("meditating"), when his astral-form was transferred to a gigantic UFO that was sitting in Earth-orbit, and where he met a group of aliens know as the Council of Seven Lights, who bestowed upon him the usual Space-Brotherly spiel about humankind's forever-wicked ways.

One of those who had the opportunity to see Van Tassel in action during this time frame, as he meditated and called upon the Space-Brothers, was the Reverend Robert Short—one of the last-surviving members of the original Contactee clan of the 1950s. It was one particular evening in 1952 when Short felt compelled to drive from his Arizona home to California, in search of the "man underneath the 'big rock' [who] talked to space people" (Short, 2003).

Short believes that discarnate alien voices directed him to Giant Rock, with the intention of ensuring that he crossed paths with Van Tassel. In a fashion that would be the envy of Contactee disciples everywhere, on arriving at Giant Rock late at night, Short was invited by Van Tassel's wife to attend one of her husband's meditations—an invitation that Short was, of course, most keen to accept. Short says that both he and Van Tassel entered into altered states that historic night and received alien-driven messages concerning atomic weaponry and peace and goodwill.

In addition, Short states that, on the evening of October 10, 1958, in Paradise Valley, California, he came face-to-face with "a saucer-shaped object hovering just above the ground…approximately 35 feet in diameter and about 20 feet tall." From the craft came a "being" approximately: "…5 foot 10 inches with a well-chiseled face, high cheekbones and shoulder-length hair that blew slightly in the breeze" (Short, 2003).

The entity told Short, "We had to come down to make an adjustment in the power of our craft;" before finally returning to the other-worldly vehicle and soaring off into the night-sky. Unsurprisingly, Short's world was utterly rearranged; as a result, he became, and still continues to be, a valiant flyer of the Contactee flag (Ibid.).

Giant Rock, north of Landers, California, beneath which Contactee George Van Tassel channeled the Space-Brothers. Photo courtesy of Nick Redfern.

Meanwhile, back to Van Tassel: In August 1953, Van Tassel asserted, he finally met the aliens in the flesh; just like George Adamski's cosmic visitors, Van Tassel's extraterrestrial friends also hailed from Venus. At this historic meeting, the aliens supposedly confided in Van Tassel the means by which the average human lifespan could be massively extended. Thus was born the Integratron: a white-colored, 16-sided, two-story domed building that supposedly had the ability to recharge and rejuvenate body-cells, potentially ad infinitum, the construction of which Van Tassel worked tirelessly on for years.

The principal workings of the Integratron were two fold: The first revolved around the reported sacred geometry of domes, and their apparent ability to focus upon mystical energies that emanated from within the depths of the planet. The second principle held that each and every one of us has our very own "wavelength," and that the numerous wavelengths that emanated from the Integratron would resonate with ours—the result of which would be a steady and constant recharging of basic cellular structure. That's right: By combining sacred geometry with our own mysterious "wavelengths," potential immortality was right around the corner. The Integratron was finally completed in 1959—and as evidence of the Van Tassel's undoubted skills, it was built entirely out of wood and concrete, and without the benefit of even a single nail or screw.

Van Tassel had other plans of an alien-nature up his sleeve, too. From 1953 to 1978, he organized the annual Giant Rock Spacecraft Convention that, at its height, attracted audiences in excess of 10,000, and such guest-speakers as Truman Bethurum, Orfeo Angelucci, and George Adamski. He also founded the Ministry of Universal Wisdom and the College of Universal Wisdom that acted as a vessel for the many and varied messages that he claimed to receive—via the means of "psychic resonance"—from his space-buddies. But, just as was the case with Adamski, it is from Van Tassel's FBI surveillance file (of 1953 to 1965) that we get to see a real insight into the mind, beliefs, and cosmic career of the man himself.

According to the FBI, following his early encounters with aliens, Van Tassel prepared the premier edition of his Proceedings of the College of Universal Wisdom, a self-published newsletter that operated as a vehicle for not only Van Tassel but for his alien contacts, too. In the first issue, two of Van Tassel's extraterrestrial contacts "Desca" and "Rondolla," suggested that Van Tassel's disciples "remove the binding chains of limit on your minds, throw out the barriers of fear [and] dissipate the selfishness of individual desire to attain physical and material things" (FBI, 1953).

The FBI recorded that in the edition of the Proceedings dated December 1, 1953, Van Tassel had said that a "message was received from the beings who operate the spacecraft," with orders from Ashtar, 'the Commandant of Space Station Schare' to contact Air Force Intelligence at Wright-Patterson Air Force Base, Dayton, Ohio" (Ibid.).

The FBI noted, with a mixture of concern and puzzlement at the odd nature of the affair, that Van Tassel then loftily told the Air Force: "The present destructive plans formulated for offensive and defensive war are known to us in their entirety...the present trend toward destructive war will not be interfered with by us, unless the condition warrants our

interference in order to secure this solar system. This is a friendly warning"
(FBI, 1953).

Not long afterward, a Yucca Valley resident wrote to the FBI and asked
an intriguing question: Had the Bureau considered the theory that Van
Tassel might be an undercover spy in the employ of the Soviet Union? Up
until then, the FBI probably had not, but it didn't waste any time trying
to find out. On November 12, 1954, Major S. Avner of the Air Force's
Office of Special Investigations had a meeting with N.W. Philcox—an FBI
point of liaison with the Air Force—to discuss the growing controversy
surrounding Van Tassel. Several days after, Avner once again spoke with
Philcox, and informed him that the Air Technical Intelligence Center at
Wright-Patterson Air Force Base "has information on Van Tassel indicating
that he has corresponded with them regarding flying saucers" (FBI, 1954).
Within the corridors of power, things were beginning to heat up.

The Air Force's statement was very likely in reference to the missive
that Van Tassel penned to ATIC on the orders of Ashtar. As a result, and
not surprisingly, the Air Force offered "to furnish the Bureau with more
detailed information" (FBI, 1954). One day after Major Avner engaged
Philcox in discussion, two dark-suited representatives of the FBI spent a
memorable morning driving across the harsh deserts of California to meet
with Van Tassel in his underground lair at Giant Rock. In a document
dated November 16, 1954, the following was noted, in typically straight-
laced, bureaucratic fashion:

> Relative to spacemen and space craft, VAN TASSEL declared
> that a year ago last August, while sleeping out of doors with his wife
> in the Giant Rock area, and at about 2.00 a.m. he was awakened by
> a man from space. This individual spoke English and was dressed
> in a grey one-piece suit similar to a sweat suit in that it did not have
> any buttons, pockets, and noticeable seams. This person, according
> to VAN TASSEL, invited him to inspect a spacecraft or flying
> saucer, which had landed on Giant Rock airstrip. VAN TASSEL
> claimed the craft was bell shaped resembling a saucer. He further
> described the ship as approximately 35 feet in diameter and is now
> known as the scout type craft. Aboard this craft was located three
> other male individuals wearing the same type of dress and identical
> in every respect with earth people.

The FBI continued:

VAN TASSEL claims that the three individuals aboard the craft were mutes in that they could not talk. He claimed they conversed through thought transfers, and also operated the flight of the craft through thought control. He stated that the spokesman for the group claimed he could talk because he was trained by his family to speak. The spokesman stated that earthmen are using too much metal in their everyday work and are fouling up radio frequencies and thought transfers because of this over use of metal. According to VAN TASSEL, these individuals came from Venus and are by no means hostile nor do they intend to harm this country or inhabitants in any manner. He declared they did not carry weapons, and the spacecraft was not armed. He mentioned that a field of force was located around the spacecraft which would prohibit anything known to earth men to penetrate. VAN TASSEL claims this craft departed from the earth after 20 minutes and has not been taken back since.

Van Tassel, the FBI agents said, had told them that "through thought transfers with space men," he had been able to ascertain that a third world war was on the horizon, which was going to be "large" and "destructive"; that this could be confirmed in the pages of The Bible; and that the "space people are peace loving and under no circumstances would enter or provoke a war."

With that duly recorded, the two FBI agents turned their attentions towards Van Tassel's written output:

In connection with his metaphysical religion and research, he publishes bi-monthly a publication in the form of a booklet called PROCEEDINGS OF THE COLLEGE OF UNIVERSAL WISDOM, YUCCA VALLEY, CALIFORNIA. He declared this publication is free and has grown from an original mailing list of 250 to 1,000 copies. VAN TASSEL stated that he sends his publication to various individuals, Universities, and Government Agencies throughout the world. He declared this publication is forwarded to the Federal Bureau of Investigation at Washington, D.C. He stated that he has donated 10 acres of his ranch holdings to the college. He mentioned that many of the buildings will be made free of metal; which will be keeping within the request of the spacemen.

Intriguingly, the FBI was particularly interested in determining who, precisely, was providing the money to allow Van Tassel's activities to flourish:

[Van Tassel] declared that for the most part he secures money for his needs of life, for the furtherance of his religion, research, and college through the generosity of certain individuals, number about 100. He failed to identify any of these people. He also mentioned that he derives income from his airstrip and a very small restaurant which is located at Giant Rock.

VAN TASSEL voluntarily stated that he is not hiding anything nor is he doing anything against the laws of this country in his research at Giant Rock. He voluntarily mentioned that he is a loyal American and would be available at any time to assist the Bureau. VAN TASSEL did not volunteer the names of any individuals whom he was soliciting for funds except his statement above that he sent his publications to various individuals, universities and Government agencies and also the Federal Bureau of Investigation in Washington, DC (FBI, 1954).

With the unusual interview at a close, the agents asked Van Tassel if they might take a few issues of his journal back to their workplace for additional review. A delighted Van Tassel was more than happy to enlighten the pair; he even secured the postal address of their particular FBI office, and agreed to mail them copies of all his future publications on the Space Brothers—which he did. Although, whether he would have done so had he known those same journals were being secretly scrutinized by agents who were on the lookout for Soviet sympathizers, is a matter that will now remain forever unanswered.

In April 1960, Van Tassel delivered a lengthy lecture at the Phipps Auditorium, in Denver, Colorado, having been offered the opportunity to do so by the Denver Unidentified Flying Objects Investigative Society. Although neither the society nor Van Tassel knew it, an agent of the FBI was present to carefully note every word, every syllable, and every nuance. As evidence of this, we have the following, extensive FBI report:

The program consisted of a 45 minute movie which included several shots of things purported to be flying saucers, and then a number of interviews with people from all walks of life regarding sightings they had made of such unidentified flying objects. After the movie GEORGE W. VAN TASSEL gave a lecture which was more of a religious-economics lecture than one of unidentified flying objects.

VAN TASSEL stated that he had been in the 'flying game' for over 30 years and currently operates a private Civil Aeronautics Authority approved airfield in California. He said he has personally observed a good many sightings and has talked to hundreds of people who have also seen flying saucers. He said that he has also been visited by the people from outer space and has taken up the cause of bringing the facts of these people to the American people. He said it is a crusade which he has undertaken because he is more or less retired, his family is grown and gone from home, and he feels he might be doing some good by this work.

The major part of his lecture was devoted to explaining the occurrences in the Bible as they related to the space people. He said that the only mention of God in the Bible is in the beginning when the universe was being made. He said that after that all references are to 'out of the sky' or 'out of heaven.'

He said that this is due to the fact that man, space people, was made by God [sic] and that in the beginning of the world the space people came to the Earth and left animals here. These were the prehistoric animals which existed at a body temperature of 105 degrees; however a polar tilt occurred whereby the poles shifted and the tropical climates became covered with ice and vice versa.

After the polar tilt the temperature to sustain life was 98.6 degrees, which was suitable for space people, so they established a colony and left only males here, intending to bring females at a latter date on supply ships. This is reflected in Adam not having a wife. He said that Adam was not an individual but a race of men.

[Van Tassel] said that this race then inter-married with 'intelligent, upright walking animals,' which race was EVE [sic]. Then when the space people came back in the supply ships they saw what had happened and did not land but ever since due to the origin of ADAM, they have watched over the people on Earth.

He said that this is in the Bible many times, such as MOSES receiving the Ten Commandments. He said the Ten Commandments are the laws of the space people and men on earth only give them lip service. Also, the manna from heaven was bread supplied by the space people.

He also stated that this can be seen from the native stories such as the Indians in America saying that corn and potatoes, unknown in Europe were brought here by a 'flaming canoe.' He said that this can be shown also by the old stories of Winged Chariots and Winged white Horses, which came from out of the sky.

He said that JESUS was born of MARY, who was a space person sent here already pregnant in order to show the earth people the proper way to live. He said the space people have watched over us through the years and have tried to help us. He said they have sent their agents to the earth and they appear just as we do; however, they have the power to know your thoughts just as JESUS did. He said this is their means of communication and many of the space people are mute, but they train a certain number of them to speak earth languages.

Van Tassel said that the space people here on earth are equipped with a 'crystal battery' which generates a magnetic field about them which bends light waves so that they, the space people, appear invisible. He said this has resulted in ghost stories, such as footsteps, doors opening, and other such phenomena" (FBI, 1960).

Almost certainly, the main concern for the FBI with regard to Van Tassel was the potential effect that his comments on nuclear war would have on the populace. This is borne out by the following section of the file which had the word *Important* handwritten at the start of the summary:

[T]he space people are now gravely concerned with our atom bombs. [Van Tassel] said that the explosions of these bombs have upset the Earth's rotation and, as in the instance of the French bomb explosion in North Africa, have actually caused earthquakes. He said that the officials on Earth are aware of this and this was the reason for the recent Geophysical Year in order to try to determine just what can be done. He said these explosions are forcing the Earth toward another polar tilt, which will endanger all mankind.

He said that the space people are prepared to evacuate those Earth people who have abided by the 'Golden Rule' when the polar tilt occurs, but will leave the rest to perish.

He advised that the space people have contacted the officials on Earth and have advised them of their concern but this has not been made public. He also said that the radioactive fallout has become extremely dangerous and officials are worried but each power is so greedy of their own power they will not agree to make peace. Van Tassel also spent some time saying that the US Air Force, who are [sic] responsible for investigations on unidentified flying objects, has suppressed information; and as they are responsible only to the Administration, not to the public, as elected officials are, they can get away with this. He said that also the Air Force is afraid that they will be outmoded and disbanded if such information gets out. The Administration's main concern in not making public any information is that the economy will be ruined, not because of any fear that would be engendered in the public. He said this is due to the number of scientific discoveries already made and that will be made which are labor saving and of almost permanency so that replacements would not be needed (FBI, 1960).

Summing up, the unknown FBI agent recorded:

Throughout his lecture, VAN TASSEL mentioned only the U.S. economy and Government and the U.S. Air Force. He did refer to the human race numerous times but all references to Government and economy could only be taken as meaning the U.S. One question put to him was whether sightings had been made in Russia or China. He answered this by saying sightings had been reported all over the world, but then specifically mentioned only the U.Ss, Australia, New Zealand, and New Guinea. He also mentioned that he was not advocating or asking for any action on the part of the audience because he said evil has a way of destroying itself. He did say that he felt that the audience, of about 250 persons, were the only intelligent people in Denver and he knew they had not come out of curiosity but because they wanted to do the right thing. He said that they were above average in intelligence and when the critical time came, the world would need people such as this to think and guide (FBI, 1960).

But the FBI's surveillance of Van Tassel was not yet complete. In April 1965, the FBI's Miami office became the recipient of wild tales to the effect that Van Tassel had constructed a device that could render people blind. According to the FBI's initial inquiries, "an ultra-rightist with tendency toward violence," who was known to Van Tassel, was somehow implicated in the story, too (FBI, 1965). A memorandum to FBI headquarters at Washington, D.C., summarized the weird saga:

A source, who has furnished reliable information in the past, and in addition has furnished information which could not be verified or corroborated, advised that a secret device, which can be carried on a person and used to blind people, has recently been perfected. This device, also referred to by [censored] as a weapon, formerly developed to keep others from seeing operator of weapon. [Censored] reports no other details regarding description and use of device. However, he said his information was second hand.

The source states that it has been determined the alleged device, was developed by GEORGE W. VAN TASSEL, Giant Rock, Yucca Valley, California, who reportedly owns or operates an airport some 20 miles from Yucca Valley in the desert area. Source stated VAN TASSEL claimed he worked over seven years in research and development of this device and the machine to make it. The weapon reportedly is of an electrical type, not further described. Any additional information can be obtained only by individuals who purchase the device and must be present at the time it is made (FBI, 1965).

Seven days later, the FBI seemed less interested in pursuing the matter:

"Because of Van Tassel's apparent mental condition, as evidenced by his statements and apparent beliefs concerning interplanetary travel by men from Venus, and in view of his other highly imaginative and incredible statements concerning space travel and population, it is believed that no further inquiries need be conducted by the Miami or Los Angeles Offices concerning Van Tassel" (Ibid.).

George Van Tassel's Integratron-still standing after more than 50 years. Courtesy of Nick Redfern.

The FBI's concerns about Van Tassel were definitely fading: He was
described in an April 12, 1965, FBI report as "an eccentric, self-ordained
minister of a quasi-religious organization." In similar vein, a several-page
memorandum of that same year, from the FBI at Los Angeles to Hoover,
came straight to the point and dubbed Van Tassel with a less-than-flattering
title: "mental case" (Ibid.).

The final document in the Bureau's dossier on Van Tassel is a letter of
August 17, 1965, from a member of the public expressing the belief that
Van Tassel's proclamations concerning flying saucers were not conducive
to the well-being of the nation: "In my opinion, it is quite subversive and
in conflict with the interests of the United States the way this gentleman
uses the demoralizing of religion and also his accusations against our
Government" (Ibid.). The FBI, apparently tired of Van Tassel and his
alien-allies, failed to act on this matter, and neither Van Tassel nor the

details of his alleged adventures with the Space-Brothers ever again graced the pages of their secret files. But his time within the weird world of UFOs was not quite over.

Van Tassel continued to hold his annual conferences up until the 1970s, but the golden years were already long gone, as UFO authority Jim Moseley notes: "…what killed it by 1970 was that there were a lot of hard-ass bikers showing up, raising hell and it wasn't the sort of gentle, new age crowd that [Van Tassel] was catering to, and he sort of got tired of it. California bikers you don't mess with. But while it was going it was a wonderful circus" (Bishop, 1995).

Van Tassel died on February 9, 1978, at the age of 67—after which there were plans to turn the Integratron into a discotheque, something that would undoubtedly have had Van Tassel spinning in his grave like a veritable top had it come to pass. It was not to be, however. The Integratron stands today much as it did all those decades ago: still a magnet for those that wish to commune with the denizens of other realms, rejuvenate their bodies, and meditate in the same, precise fashion that Van Tassel did way back at the turn of the 1950s. As evidence of its staying power, the Integratron even survived the mighty force of an earthquake of 7.3 magnitude that rattled and shook the area in 1992.

There is one, final thought-provoking aspect to the saga of George Van Tassel that is worthy of mention: On the morning of February 23, 2000, a sizeable chunk of Giant Rock broke off and came crashing to the ground—an event that was seen by local shamans as the fulfilment of an old prophecy that had longed been anticipated by the ancient natives of nearby Joshua Tree. So the legend went with respect to Giant Rock: "…the day when the Mother would split open…a new era would be revealed." That era, it was suggested by the shamans, related to the so-called "Divine Feminine," throughout which compassion and peace would eventually reign supreme (Labyrinthina, 2007). The calamity at Giant Rock was evidence, in some shamanic quarters at least, that the era in question had finally begun.

Perhaps George Van Tassel was right after all. Maybe kindly and benevolent extraterrestrials really were trying to put the planet to rights, and he was a part of their cosmic plans. And, just possibly, they really did choose Giant Rock as their world-saving focal point.

7

Alternative
Aliens

Although the cases discussed thus far are without doubt controversial in the extreme, they at least share one common factor: they all focus upon alien contact of a type that we have come to accept as being somewhat logical—that of extraterrestrial visitors landing on our world in futuristic spacecraft and making their presence known to the chosen elite. But what should we make of those Contactee-style events in which the aliens supposedly revealed themselves not at the base of some huge flying saucer, but by distinctly alternative means, including via the medium of Morse Code, within the pleasant confines of a London apartment, and while their intended target was blissfully washing dishes in his kitchen? Some might say that such tales are beyond ludicrous—but when those same tales involve a senior figure within the British military and agents of the CIA, perhaps we should not be so quick to dismiss them.

George King was born in Shropshire, England, in 1919 to parents George and Mary, and went on to become one of the most well-known of all the Contactees of the 1950s and 1960s. Even from a young age, King was surrounded by high-strangeness. His mother and grandmother claimed to be psychics; and, in his book *You Too Can Heal*, King related how, at the age of 11, and while his mother was seriously ill and confined to bed, he headed deep into the heart of nearby woods, where he prayed intently for her speedy recovery. As King did so, an angelic being appeared before him, instructed him to return home, and informed him that his mother was now fully cured. After excitedly racing home and learning that she was indeed restored to full health, a realization came to King that his life was not at all like the lives of the other kids in the neighborhood.

At the outbreak of the Second World War, King—a "conscientious objector" who refused to fight against Hitler's hordes—took a position in London with the National Fire Service. By the time hostilities were at a close, King was in his 20s, and had begun to develop a deep interest in yoga, alternative therapies, and new age style belief systems. This radical change in the mindset of King came to the fore on a Saturday morning in May 1954, when, while doing nothing stranger than washing dishes in his Maida Vale, London, apartment, he heard a loud, disembodied voice cry out, "Prepare yourself! You are to become the voice of Interplanetary Parliament!" (Aetherius Society, 2006).

Allegedly, in the immediate aftermath, said King, he became the recipient of countless channeled messages, from a "great Yogi adept" who materialized in his apartment and warned him of "the unfeeling march of science into the realms of the atom." Further messages came from a highly spiritual, Venusian being named Aetherius, who bestowed a wealth of words of wisdom upon the shocked-but-elevated King. So elevated by the cosmic experiences was King that he quickly quit his job as a taxi-driver and established the Aetherius Society, believing that space-aliens held "the key to the salvation both of the planet as a whole and of every individual on Earth" (Wikipedia, 2009).

On July 23, 1958, King claimed a close encounter with none other than Jesus Christ atop Holdstone Down—a 330-meter-high hill above the village of Combe Martin, in the English county of Devonshire. So the story went, 13 days earlier, King received a channeled message from Aetherius, who advised him to travel to Combe Martin, where he would receive instructions from an "adept from Mars." Seeing absolutely nothing strange in this, King dutifully did as he was told. Sure enough, upon taking his position on Holdstone Down he could see a "blue sphere" hovering over the waters of the Bristol Channel, after which Jesus—dressed in a flowing and glowing robe, and sporting a wand—came into view.

Researchers Dr. David Clarke and Andy Roberts say: "Waves of energy passed between the entity and King who was plunged into a religious rapture before 'Jesus' stepped into a beam of light and vanished. King realized that Holdstone Down was now charged, a spiritual power battery whose energies were inexhaustible" (Clarke, 2007).

It seems King's own energies were inexhaustible, too: One year later, he founded an American branch of the Aetherius Society—in Los Angeles, where King ultimately moved to live permanently, and where he enthusiastically continued to spread the words of wisdom bestowed upon him by various other-worldly entities with whom he claimed to have communed. George King suffered a heart-attack in 1986, underwent a multiple heart bypass in 1992, and died in Santa Barbara on July 12, 1997. The Aetherius Society continues to thrive.

Born in 1921, Air Marshal Sir Beresford Peter Torrington Horsley embarked upon an illustrious career with the British military in 1939, when he took a position as deck-boy on the *TSS Cyclops*, a steamer bound for Malaya. For the return journey, and as the Second World War was declared, he changed ships—to the *TSS Menelaus*, and eventually gravitated to a career in the Royal Air Force: first as an air-gunner, then as a pilot, and subsequently as a flight instructor.

Horsley was later attached to the Communications-Squadron of the 2nd Tactical Air Force in France, and, during the D-Day invasion of Normandy, he accepted the job of personal pilot to Major-General Sir Miles Graham. He returned to England in 1947, joined the staff of the Central Flying School, 23 Training Group, and was appointed Adjutant to the Oxford University Air Squadron in 1948.

In July 1949, Horsley entered the Royal Household as a Squadron Leader, and as Equerry to Her Royal Highness, the Princess Elizabeth, Duchess of Edinburgh (better known today as Her Majesty, Queen Elizabeth II), and to His Royal Highness, the Duke of Edinburgh. In 1952, Horsley became a Wing-Commander and in 1953 became a full-time Equerry to the Duke of Edinburgh, a role he held until 1956.

From the latter part of the 1950s to the early 1960s, Horsley was employed as Senior-Instructor at the RAF Flying College, Manby, Lincolnshire; as Commanding-Officer at RAF Wattisham, Suffolk; and as Group-Captain, Near-East Air Force (NEAF), Operations, on the island of Cyprus. Horsley made the rank of Air Vice-Marshal, later attaining the position of Assistant-Chief of Air-Staff (Operations), and then that of Commanding-Officer, 1-Group from 1971 to 1973. His final post in the Royal Air Force was as the Deputy-Commander-in-Chief of Strike Command, which he held from 1973 to 1975. Horsley's other claim to fame is that he had a face-to-face encounter with a human-looking alien who went by the memorable name of Mr. Janus.

The strange affair began when Horsley learned of the Duke of Edinburgh's fascination with the complexities of the UFO puzzle. According to Horsley, "He was quite interested. As always, his mind was open. He agreed I should do a study on the subject in my spare time; as long as I kept it in perspective and didn't bring the Palace into disrepute. He didn't want to see headlines about him believing in little green men" (*Daily Mail*, 1997).

With typical British understatement, Horsley said, "At the end of my tour at the Palace, I had a very strange experience" (Ibid.)

Sir Arthur Barratt, who worked at Buckingham Palace as Gentleman Usher to the Sword of State, introduced Horsley to a mysterious "General Martin," who, in turn put him in touch with an "enigmatic" Mrs. Markham. Interestingly, English researchers Dr. David Clarke and Andy Roberts learned from Horsley that General Martin "believed UFOs were visitors from an alien civilization which wanted to warn us of the dangers posed by atomic war" (Clarke, 2007). According to Horsley, it was Markham who told him to turn up at a particular apartment in London's Chelsea district on a specific evening, where he met a stranger who introduced himself only as Mr. Janus.

Horsley said of his chat with the man that: "Janus was there, sitting by the fire in a deep chair. He asked: 'What is your interest in flying saucers?' We talked for hours about traveling in space and time. I don't know what or who he was. He didn't say he was a visitor from another planet but I had that impression. I believe he was here to observe us. I never saw him again. I have no qualms about the reaction to my experience with Mr. Janus" (*Daily Mail*, 1997).

Rather disturbingly, and echoing the claims of so many of the Contactees that the Space-Brothers were concerned by our ever-growing nuclear arsenals, UFO investigator Timothy Good says: "In my second and last meeting with Sir Peter Horsley at his home in 2000, he revealed that, in addition to being disturbed by the realization that Janus was reading his mind, he was even more disturbed by the fact that this extraordinary man 'knew all Britain's top-secret nuclear secrets'" (Good, 2007).

Is it possible that this bizarre episode was actually part of some state-sponsored operation designed to ascertain the nature of Sir Peter's character and his loyalty to the country? This particularly novel theory was most assuredly on the minds of researchers Clarke and Roberts, who asked Horsley if he considered it feasible that he had been "set up" by MI5 (the British equivalent of the FBI) to "test his vulnerability." Horsley provided the pair with an adamant "no" (Clarke, 2007).

Right up until his death in 2001, Horsley's position on the overwhelmingly weird experience was rock-solid: "I don't care what people think—it was what happened. I would say they come from another planet somewhere in the universe but not in our galaxy. They are benign, not aggressive and, like us, are explorers" (*Daily Mail*, 1997).

In 1955, two aging sisters in Chicago, Mildred and Marie Maier— who, decades earlier, had been minor figures in the world of theater— contacted the *Journal of Space Flight* to relate their apparent experiences with, and evidence of, flying saucers. That evidence allegedly included an alien "code" that had been broadcast during a radio show that the sisters had the presence of mind to tape when things started to turn weird on-air. As the story took hold, other ham-radio operators claimed to have heard the uncanny "space message," too. Then something decidedly intriguing occurred: None other than the CIA's Office of Scientific Intelligence (OSI) sat up and took notice—albeit clandestinely. As a direct result, Mildred and Marie became the focus of much attention by the CIA, the OSI, and its Scientific Contact Branch.

CIA field officers, one of who was a man named Dewelt Walker, established contact with the Maier sisters, who were said to be "thrilled that the government was interested," (Haines, 1997) and arranged a time and day to meet with them. In trying to hide any evidence of CIA interest in the affair, Walker rashly passed himself off as an employee of the Air Force, something that came back to haunt the CIA a couple of years later. In trying to secure the potentially groundbreaking tape-recording, CIA personnel recorded—with a great deal of justification, it might be said— that they had stumbled upon a scene highly reminiscent of *Arsenic and Old Lace*.

"The only thing lacking was the elderberry wine," Walker humorously advised his colleagues (Haines, 1997). After valiantly pretending to take an interest in the sisters' bulging scrapbook of faded and yellowing clippings from their bygone days as entertainers on the stage, the somewhat bemused, amused and confused CIA agents successfully obtained a copy of the potentially priceless recording. Alas, the whole affair had a far more down-to-earth explanation, however: OSI personnel carefully analyzed the recording and were quickly able to determine that this was no message from the Space-Brothers. Rather, it was nothing stranger than Morse code from an unnamed radio station somewhere in the United States. There the matter duly rested until 1957, when a persistent bloodhound of a UFO researcher named Leon Davidson entered the story and began talking enthusiastically with the Maier sisters. Mildred and Marie—once again overjoyed to be the center of attention—advised Davidson of their conversation with "Mr. Walker of the Air Force."

Hot on the trail, and sensing a cover-up, Davidson quickly penned a letter to the mysterious Dewelt Walker, believing him to be an Air Force Intelligence Officer from Wright-Patterson, to ask if the tape had been analyzed at ATIC. Somewhat surprisingly, Walker himself actually replied to Davidson, and advised him that the recording had been forwarded to the proper authorities for evaluation and study, and that no further information was available concerning the results.

Of course, this was precisely the sort of reply that was guaranteed to raise Davidson's hackles and put him hot on the trail of the truth. Far from happy with Walker's reply, and very astutely suspecting that Walker was nothing less than an employee of the CIA, Davidson fired off a letter to none other than Allen Dulles, the Director of Central Intelligence himself, loftily demanding to know what the coded message actually meant and who Mr. Walker really was. The CIA, quite naturally wanting to keep Walker's identity as a CIA employee an overwhelming secret, replied that another official agency had analyzed the tape in question and that Davidson would be hearing directly from the Air Force.

On August 5, 1957, the Air Force rather foolishly kept up the pretense, and wrote to Davidson, earnestly stating (yet lying through its teeth) that Walker "was and is an Air Force Officer" and that the tape "was analyzed by another government organization" (Haines, 1997). The Air Force's letter asserted that the recording of the Maier sisters contained nothing stranger than Morse code. Far from satisfied, Davidson wrote to Dulles again. This time he wanted to know the full identity of the Morse code operator, and of the agency that had conducted the analysis. As a result of their somewhat absurd chicanery, both the CIA and the Air Force found themselves in a deep quagmire—and all as a result of their unusual interest in the rather bizarre beliefs and activities of two little old ladies.

Then things got even more confusing: CIA officers, firmly undercover, contacted Davidson and assured him they would get the code translated, as well as, hopefully, a positive identification of the transmitter. In yet another attempt to pacify the Sherlock Holmes–style Davidson, a CIA officer, under cover and wearing an Air Force uniform, contacted Davidson.

The CIA officer assured Davidson that there really was no "super agency" involved in the investigation of the UFO mystery, and that the Air Force's policy was not to disclose who was doing what. Davidson was not one to be easily thwarted: He continued to press for disclosure of both the recording and its source. The officer reluctantly agreed to see what he could do. After checking in with headquarters, the CIA officer phoned Davidson to report that a thorough check had been made and, because the signal was known to be of American origin, the tape and the notes made at the time had been conveniently destroyed to conserve file-space.

Unsurprisingly furious over what he perceived (quite correctly, as it transpired) as a definitive runaround, Davidson told the CIA officer that "he and his agency, whichever it was, were acting like Jimmy Hoffa and the Teamster Union in destroying records which might indict them" (Haines, 1997). Anticipating that any further debate with Davidson would only serve to create even more speculation, the Contact Division utterly washed its hands of the issue by reporting to the Director of Central Intelligence, and to the Air Force's Air Technical Intelligence Center, that under no circumstances would it ever respond to or try to contact Davidson again. Thus, a very minor, and rather bizarre incident, handled surprisingly amateurishly by both CIA and the Air Force, turned into a major flap that added fuel to the growing mystery surrounding contacts from space.

As laughable as this farcical episode most assuredly was, it presents more clues into the inner-workings of the CIA, and its relationship with the UFO mystery, than the Agency would perhaps prefer. For example, the surreal saga shows that the CIA was not above passing its agents off as employees of other agencies as it attempted to gain possession of UFO data and determine what the Maier sisters had come across. That the two elderly sisters had probably stumbled upon nothing more sinister than a Morse code transmission, rather than a message from the Space-Brothers, is far less important than the fact that the CIA went to great levels to get its hands on the recording—and in a distinctly clandestine fashion, too.

In view of this, we might very well ponder upon this final intriguing question before moving on to pastures new: Was the CIA's pressing determination to (a) get hold of Mildred and Marie's recording at all costs, and (b) blatantly lie and obfuscate about who its agents were working for, prompted by a possibility that this was not the first time that stories of aliens contacting the human race via the medium of radio had secretly reached the eyes and ears of the CIA?

8

"I am Diane. I come from Venus."

One of the most puzzling aspects of the Contactee controversy is that the overwhelming majority of those who claimed interaction with human-like extraterrestrials were male. But that does not mean that the significantly smaller number of reports involving women were of any less importance. Arguably, the exact opposite is the case. Researcher Gavin Gibbons wrote in 1957 that one October evening in 1954, a Dutchman living in England named Tony Roestenberg returned home to find his wife, Jessie, "in a terrified state." According to Jessie, earlier that day a flying saucer had hovered over their isolated farmhouse at the village of Ranton, Staffordshire. In addition, Jessie could see peering down from the craft two very "Nordic"-like men that could have stepped right out of the pages of *Flying Saucers Have Landed*: their foreheads were high, their hair was long, and they seemed to have "pitiful" looks on their faces. The strange craft reportedly circled the family's home twice, before streaking away. Curiously, on the following Sunday, Tony Roestenberg had a "hunch" that if he climbed on the roof of his house "he would see something unusual," which he most certainly did: a high-flying, cigar-shaped object that vanished into the clouds (Gibbons, 1957).

Gibbons, who investigated the case personally, stated: "When I visited the Roestenberg's house almost three weeks after the sighting... Jessie Roestenberg appeared. She seemed highly strained and nervous and her husband, coming in later, was also very strained. It was evident that something most unusual had occurred" (Ibid.).

Then there is the very-little-known case of Margit Mustapa, who was born and raised in Finland and who, in her youth, performed with the Helsinki National Opera. She allegedly viewed an immense cigar-shaped UFO in the skies of Seattle while visiting the city in 1950, and finally settled to live, in the early 1950s, in definitive Contactee land: California. Mustapa was the author of two books (written in 1960 and 1963 respectively): *Spaceship to the Unknown* and *Book of Brothers*. With chapter titles like "Toward the Universal Brotherhood"; "Tall Venusian Brother Appears"; "Brother of Electricity Explains"; and "Cooperation with Brotherhood," these are classic books that easily rival the written-output of Adamski, Fry, and Angelucci.

And take a look at the publisher's blurb about Mustapa's alleged encounters that appears on the jacket of *Spaceship to the Unknown*, which echoes the claims of Truman Bethurum that the Space Brothers were not averse to clandestinely operating in our cities:

"Mrs. Mustapa's men and women from other planets are not the queer, bug-eyed creatures usually pictured. Her first 'contacts' with space people were a gentle-appearing woman in an ordinary car, and a bronzed, black-haired motorist in sports garb (including a colorful Hawaiian shirt)—both encountered on a road near Los Angeles. No words were exchanged. None were necessary. Telepathic vibrations carried their message" (Mustapa, 1960).

The messages and data imparted were certainly significant. *Book of Brothers* stated: "The Brothers of this book are Venusians. They have influenced thousands of minds to understand how to grow inwardly, spiritually, and mentally toward extraplanetary [sic] dimensions in thinking…In the universal concept, each individual, through meditation and study, must find his place. But first he must free himself from traditional thinking and open his mind to the implications of the Space Age which the whirling satellites of today symbolize. To this goal the Brothers offered the spiritual key…We can become as gods, living in a new era of harmony; we can penetrate to outer space and the promise of the future…a future of love, understanding and peace" (Mustapa, 1963).

Without doubt the most well-known, and still fondly remembered, female Contactee of the 1950s was Dana Howard; a woman whose experiences researcher Regan Lee has dug into extensively. Lee says: "While I'm intrigued by the Contactees in general, and realize there are many perspectives and theories surrounding 'what really happened,' I'd like to focus on the symbolic [aspect] of Howard's experience, rather than attempt to prove or disprove her experience. What stood out for me as I read about Dana Howard's accounts were the similarities to Marian Apparitions. Howard's experiences seemed to be a blend of space age Contactee encounters, complete with flying saucers, and some of the characteristics of appearances of the Virgin Mary" (Lee, 2007).

According to Howard, her first encounter with a non-human being occurred in 1939: "Still wrapped in the warm intoxication of the spirit, my vision was directed to a gnarled, old tree overlooking the antediluvian hills. Leaning casually against the grotesque trunk was a woman being of unsurpassed loveliness. Her head was radiant with a crown of fire, strands of golden hair cascading gently over her beautiful, slightly olive-tinted shoulders. The strange mystic light flooding her dark, prophetic eyes, added a wistful something to all her other charms" (Howard, 1956).

Lee comments that this is "similar in ways to reports of seeing the entity, Mary." However, adds Lee: "the sighting turns space-age" (Lee, 2007). Indeed, it does.

Howard stated that, as the experience continued, it was complemented by her viewing of "a beautiful rocket-shaped ship suspended in mid-air about three hundred feet from the earth…In the main it seemed to be constructed of some sort of translucent materials, but trimmed in gold, and gem-studded."

Howard added that "an almost invisible 'ladder' extended from the ship to the earth" and the "radiant being" climbed the steps and vanished.

"I never saw her again," she recorded.

Or, at least not until 1955, as Regan Lee explains: "…sixteen years after the first encounter, Diane the Venusian appeared for the second time, this time during a séance. The séance was conducted by a well known medium at the time, Reverend Bertie Lillie Candler, in Los Angeles, California. An 8 foot tall female figure, described as being very beautiful, appeared before them" (Lee, 2007).

Lee takes up the story from there: "The female entity said she was the same Diane from Venus that Dana had met 16 years ago, and was responsible for giving Dana telepathic messages during that time. Like most of the other good-looking humanoid beings of the Contactee era, she imparted messages of the importance of spiritual growth, transformation of both body and psyche, and eventual life on Venus" (Ibid.).

Howard's account of the séance was memorable: "I had never attended a materialization séance before, and my inquiring mind asked all sorts of questions. As my cerebral atoms whirled with curiosity toward the close of the meeting the 'little white church' seemed to me, electrified with a powerful vibration. Then, some 10 or 12 feet from the draped-off area where Reverend Candler was in deep trance I saw a rising glow of phosphorescence. It was very tall at first, but out of this phosphorescent substance a form began to manifest itself. She was definitely different from the other 'spirit' manifestations, a solid, fleshly being, delicate in charm and manner" (Howard, 1956).

"She called for Dana. Overwhelmed with emotion I could not choke back, I went up to her, standing only inches away from the manifestation. While I did not recognize her instantly, I knew there was something quaintly familiar about her. Standing like a sylph-like goddess, and bowing low in greeting to the 27 persons present, the rich tones of her voice vibrated through the little church" (Lee, 2007).

A woman named Lucile Points, who was also present at the séance, recalled that a beautiful being "came, rather hesitantly at first, then saying, 'I am Diane. I come from Venus.' Because I was sitting next to the draped-off place I greeted this beautiful one asking: 'With whom do you wish to speak?' She replied softly: 'I wish to speak with Dana'" (Howard, 1956).

There were other witnesses, too, as Howard noted: "On April 29, 1955, the writer, Mrs. Gladys Campbell and my friend, Mrs. Maude Haas, attended a materialization séance at the Church...the medium being Reverend Bertie Lillie Candler of Florida" (Ibid.).

Campbell duly provided the following statement to Howard: "I am more than happy to give an account of what I witnessed to the best of my recollection; and you will recall, when you spoke at the Pyramid Church in Alhambra the following Sunday after the visit, I was the one who got up and verified your statements concerning the visit of Diane. It was truly a marvelous thing to be present and see for myself such a wonderful personality, and I know you must be very humble and gratified to have the facts that you brought before the public in your book, *My Flight to Venus*, substantiated in such an unexpected manner" (Lee, 2007).

Regan Lee notes astutely: "It's interesting Diane said she came from Venus; for Venus, of course, is the planet representing the female sex, fertility, beauty, love. It is the morning and the evening star" (Ibid.).

Diane most certainly did provide Howard with messages of love: "Child of Earth," Diane said, "try to listen through space for the voice of one who has not forgotten. Try to make every breath, a breath of love. Try to make every word a word of love. Make every act an act of love. To do so, is to love and be loved. When you find the great jewel of love in your heart, you will find also, as you walk down the streets of life, the good and the noble in every soul you meet" (Ibid.).

Expanding on this issue, Lee points out that: "The name Diane, a form of Diana, means the Divine. So we have a Divine Love from the heavens, appearing to an earthling with messages of love, creativity, and the need for constructive transformation; raising the self up to a higher vibration. The symbolism in these encounters is interesting. Was it a true encounter with an alien? Or the same presence that is manifest in appearances of the Virgin

Mary? It is interesting the experience took place during a séance; a perfect setting for manifestations of all kinds of spirits and entities; including some part of Dana Howard herself that was Diane. We don't know, and probably never will know, if Dana Howard's experiences were some kind of liminal, paranormal experience, or if she made the whole thing up" (Ibid.).

Lee stresses, however: "Whatever 'really' happened, the Dana Howard encounter is certainly a highly interesting case" (Ibid.).

It was, as Greg Bishop has also noted: "In the heavily male-dominated world of 1950s America, Howard stands out in a field where Contactees often lingered on descriptions of their encounters with shapely space babes" (Bishop, 2008).

Now we come to a British woman named Mollie Thompson. Researcher Simon Murphy says: "Mollie was introduced to UFOs through Desmond Leslie and George Adamski's book *Flying Saucers Have Landed* in the early 1950s. 'It spoke to me, it tweaked a nerve that I couldn't resist,' she said. Adamski's tales of advanced and beneficent aliens merged with her established interests in spiritualism and reincarnation, and the nascent new age movement. She met Adamski himself on his last trip to the U.K. in 1963—'The Brothers have work for you' he told her" (Murphy, 2009).

Investigative writers Andy Roberts and Dr. David Clarke say: "Just what that work was would soon become clear to Mollie." It appears that the Space-Brothers wished Thompson to help get their messages of peace, love, and harmony over to the public via the medium of music. In 2005, Thompson told Roberts and Clarke: "…words and music dropped into my mind. At first I thought it was my imagination, but I did begin to write them down. They fit together. I somehow knew they were going to be a song. And it was a result of these thoughts that were coming into my head, because I thought I've got to do something, they're not just given to me to play with, I've got to use them somehow, but how?" (Clarke, 2007).

The answer was simple: She made a record; a full-length album, no less, titled *From Worlds Afar*. Greg Bishop says of her recordings: "The sincerity and innocence of Thompson's feelings come through with every note. The song, *Cockeyed Ballad*, tells of her contact with the gentle space people.

Thompson describes them in a couple of lines: 'They wear one-piece suits. You can't see any seams. But apart from that, they're just like us'" (2009).

A more fitting description of the Space-Brothers would be hard to find.

9

Prince Uccelles

On June 10, 1959, Special Agents at FBI Headquarters, Washington, D.C., recorded, in a four-page document, what was possibly the strangest Contactee-related story to have ever crossed their collective desks. Titled *Interstate Transportation of Stolen Property*, the document focused upon the nefarious exploits of the black-hearted Harold Berney, whose only motivation for immersing himself in the world of the Contactee was the lure of the almighty dollar. FBI documentation on Berney's exploits began thus:

Perhaps one of the most fantastic fraudulent schemes ever to be conceived is the one in which a woman was duped into turning over between $38,000 and $40,000 of her considerable assets to an elderly man with an extraordinarily vivid imagination. Current publications contain many articles concerning travel into space and landings on the moon or one of the planets. Newspapers carry daily stories of new accomplishments in the field of astronautics and space travel forecasts. Confidence man Harold Jesse Berney, however, as early as 1952 set in motion a scheme involving alleged interplanetary travel which, by October, 1956, had defrauded his victims out of a total of $58,000.

Berney, a sign painter by trade, had a criminal record which dated back some 40 years. He was last released from prison by court order in 1949 after serving less than a year of a five-year sentence for embezzlement (FBI, 1959).

It was upon his release, the FBI related, that Berney began working on his next scam:

In 1952, Berney became active in forming the Aberney Corporation, which was intended to produce television antennae. This company was dissolved in 1953, and a year later Berney incorporated the Telewand Corporation. This company also was allegedly for the purpose of producing television antennae, but it actually served as a front for a more ambitious program its promoter had in mind.

Miss Pauline Eva Bock, a legal secretary, met Berney in the fall of 1952 and by the spring of 1953 had advanced several hundred dollars to Berney and had been made the secretary-treasurer of the Aberney Corporation, even though she was not present when elected to this position. After the Aberney Corporation went out of existence, she became secretary-treasurer of the Telewand Corporation, which was controlled entirely by Berney. Pauline Bock had no actual duties and no authority over the activities of the company or its funds (Ibid.).

Then, the FBI noted, Berney revealed to Miss Bock his utterly spurious story—that would ultimately prove tragically costly to his victim:

In the fall of 1954, Berney first began to tell Miss Bock of his trip to the planet Venus. He told her he had made a trip to Venus and had gained the confidence of certain leading men on the planet. He narrated how he had traveled to the planet on a spaceship two miles long, stopping on the moon en route, and told of his travels on the planet, his tour of the major cities, some explanation of the governmental system on Venus, and about his return to Earth after two weeks on the planet.

In his fantastic narrations of life and culture on the planet, Berney stated that apartments and office buildings on Venus dwarfed the Washington Monument. He said that little crime or dishonesty was evident because when anyone was found guilty of committing a serious crime he was just picked up and dropped off on another planet. He also stated that gold was so plentiful that it was used in the manufacture of plumbing fixtures. He went on to say that he had gone to and returned from Venus on a flying saucer and in the time it took to get there from the earth the sun had come up twice. He said that the moon was a stopping place on the way to Venus to pick up articles of trade.

Returning to his original theme, Berney related the confidence the planet's prince 'Uccelles' had in him, saying that he had been selected to supervise the manufacture on Earth of certain highly secret items which had been invented on Venus. The most important of these Berney referred to as a 'modulator,' a device which was designed to operate on energy obtained from the atmosphere and which would create greater energy potential than any atomic device (Ibid.).

In a book Berney wrote, entitled *Two Weeks on Venus*, he gave the following description of the modulator: "It not only generates power for light and manufacturing, but manufactures of itself the product known as magnetic flux, that being a source of unlimited power to operate any type of machinery" (*Time*, 1957).

FBI agents matter-of-factly noted, having read this masterfully breathtaking piece of nonsense, that: "Allegedly, the modulator could softly lift and lower millions of tons in a fraction of a second and could propel planes and spaceships at about the speed of light or hold them motionless in the sky. A modulator-equipped plane, by means of the pull of its magnetic field, could, if desired, blow every fuse in a city, stop all motors and completely block communications" (FBI, 1959).

Berney then played his ace card:

Berney told Miss Bock that he was working in conjunction with a large corporation in the East to develop the 'modulator' for use by this country. The project was so secret, he said, that the details were known only to the White House and certain top officials of the Government. For this reason, he swore her to secrecy but assured her that when the device was completed any money she had invested in it would be multiplied at least seven times.

Berney gave Pauline Bock certificates which he had signed and told her each certificate represented one share in the Telewand Corporation at $100 a share. He told her she was to take one certificate for each $100 she invested in the firm. He assured her that in order to make the stock certificates valid, it was necessary only for her to add her signature as secretary-treasurer of the firm. This she was careful to do, and she believed in the project so completely that by September, 1956, she had entrusted to Berney between $38,000 and $40,000.

One transaction between the two involved a check for the sum of $10,000 which he claimed was necessary 'to pay technicians for completing the modulator device ahead of schedule.' In addition, Berney had interested a man and his wife in his scheme to the extent that they had invested $20,000. During the period from 1954 to 1956, Berney was alleged to have made at least two trips to Venus aboard a spaceship as large as the Pentagon Building" (Ibid.).

It was not just Miss Bock that Berney was deceiving:

In the meantime, in November, 1956, it was reported that his wife and children had received word that Berney had been killed in an explosion and that there would be no burial service. His personal effects had been sent to his wife. The package also contained a camera, billfold and contents including two or three hundred dollars and all Berney's credentials.

A letter which Mrs. Berney received, supposedly from Mr. 'Uccelles' and written with a pen brush on parchment, advised her that her husband had died and that his body was lying in state on Venus. Mrs. Berney, who had not believed his tales of Venus, concluded that he had deserted her" (Ibid.).

It was not long before the authorities were in hot pursuit of this cosmic conman, as the FBI stated:

In February 1957, the information regarding Berney's defrauding operations came to the attention of the FBI and investigation was started under the Fraud by Wire Section of the Interstate Transportation of Stolen Property Statute. In the furtherance of his scheme, Berney had frequently contacted Miss Bock by telephone or letter to have her send more money to him. The check for $10,000 had been sent to him through the mail and this he had converted to his own use.

When contacted by FBI agents, Miss Bock instantly identified a photograph of Harold J. Berney as the individual who had defrauded her of her money. She said that the only things she had to show, in a material way, from Berney's schemes were a chair and a couch she got when the Telewand office was closed in 1955. She also had $800 from the sale of Telewand machinery. On March 8, 1957, authorized complaints were filed charging Berney with fraud by wire and interstate transportation of stolen property. The following day, bond was recommended for Berney at $25,000 (Ibid.).

Learning that Berney intensely disliked cold weather, FBI agents intensified their investigation in the southern states. As a result, on March 25, 1957, Berney was apprehended by an alert FBI agent at Prichard, Alabama. The agent had learned that a new sign-painting firm had recently opened in Prichard, and the agent, knowing Berney's background, had investigated and determined Berney's identity. In December 1957, Berney was sentenced to imprisonment for a term of from 20 months to five years.

It will be recalled that, according to Berney, he was in possession of a device that he called the modulator, and which, he claimed, "manufactures of itself the product known as magnetic flux," and had the ability to "blow every fuse in a city, stop all motors, and completely block communications" (FBI, 1957). This sounds not unlike the FBI's reference of January 1953 to George Adamski's knowledge of a "machine" that operated on the principle of "cutting magnetic lines of force," and that could "draw airplanes down from the sky" (FBI, 1953). The machine, Adamski told the FBI, was in the possession of a man whose name was firmly, and conveniently, excised from the FBI's Adamski file.

With the benefit of hindsight, the description of the device given to FBI agents by Adamski sounds suspiciously like that of which Berney claimed to be in possession. If it was indeed the same device, and Adamski was hanging out with a cold-hearted conman, then this does not do much at all for Adamski's credibility.

There is one final point that is more than worthy of comment, given the strange nature of the story: Pauline Eva Bock, Harold Berney's unfortunate victim, never actually existed. At least, not under that specific name: Her real name was Pauline Goebel. To protect the identity of the mortified and embarrassed woman, the files reveal, the FBI created for her an alias. Why the FBI resorted to such actions, when it could have simply blacked out Goebel's name on the declassified versions of the original files is a puzzle— but it is, nevertheless, highly appropriate for such a strange and convoluted tale.

10

Close Encounters
of the
Sexual Kind

Although Truman Bethurum's ultimate dream was undoubtedly to nail the curvy Captain Aura Rhanes of the planet Clarion, it seems that unless he left out integral aspects of his story, he never quite achieved his objective. But, only a few years after Bethurum's nighttime liaisons on Mormon Mesa, someone else finally went where, quite possibly, no man had ever gone before. That man was Antonio Villas Boas, who claimed to have been seduced by a vibrant space-babe with blood-red pubic hair and who growled like a wild beast while the pair got it on. Hey, it doesn't get much better than that, does it?

In a deposition provided to Brazilian UFO researcher Olavo Fontes on February 22, 1958, Villas Boas stated: "I am 23 years old and a farmer by profession. I live with my family on a farm which we own, near the town of Francisco de Sales, in the state of Minas Gerais, close to the border with the state of Sao Paulo." Villas Boas added that strange things were already afoot in the days leading up to his close encounter of the kinky kind: On the night of October 5, he had seen "…a very white light, and I don't know where it came from. It was as though it came from high up above, like the light of a car head-lamp shining downwards spreading its light all around…it finally went out and did not return." Nine days later, Villas Boas saw hovering over his family's property "a very bright light—so bright that it hurt the eyes—stationary at the northern end of the field…it was… approximately the size of a cart wheel [and] at a height of about 100 meters and was of a light red color, illuminating a large area of the ground" (Villas Boas, 1958).

But it was the following night that things quite literally heated up: "I was alone, plowing with the tractor at the same place," said Villas Boas. "It was a cold night and the sky was very clear, with many stars. At precisely 1 a.m., I suddenly saw a red star in the sky…In a few moments it had grown into a very luminous, egg-shaped object, flying towards me at a terrific speed. It was moving so fast that it was above the tractor before I had time to think what I should do" (Ibid.).

Villas Boas recalled that the object "suddenly halted," then "descended till it was perhaps 50 meters or so above my head, lighting up the tractor and all the ground around." Admitting that he was "terrified," Villas Boas "thought of making my escape" but concluded that his "chances of success would be slight" (Bowen, 1969). So, like the veritable deer caught in the headlights, he stood his ground, with barely a clue what to do. It would not be long, however, before matters escalated to a level that Villas Boas could not even have begun to anticipate.

"It came nearer and nearer," said Villas Boas, who added: "I was now able to see it was a strange machine, rather rounded in shape, and surrounded by little purplish lights.…[it] was like a large elongated egg with three metal spurs in front…On the upper part of the machine there was something which was revolving at great speed and also giving off a powerful fluorescent reddish light" (Ibid.).

But by Villas Boas's own admittance, it was when the strange object prepared to land that he "totally lost the little self-control that I had left." Not surprising, taking into consideration the fact that the engine of his tractor suddenly died, and he was forced to high-tail it across the fields. He did not get far, however: "...I had only run a few steps when somebody grabbed one of my arms. My pursuer was a short individual and dressed in strange clothing." Panic-stricken, Villas Boas lashed out, hitting the man and throwing him off balance. It was all to no avail, however: "I tried to use the advantage gained to continue my flight, but I was promptly attacked simultaneously by three other individuals from the sides and the rear" (Villas Boas, 1958). To his horror, Villas Boas realized their intention was to drag him aboard their vehicle—for reasons he could not imagine.

When the entities finally managed to get Villas Boas on board, they quickly stripped him down, and covered his entire body with an unidentified gel-like substance that Villas Boas described as being "as clear as water, but quite thick, and without smell." He was then led into a room where blood-samples were extracted from his chin; after which he was taken to another room, where he became acutely ill. "It was as though I was breathing a thick smoke that was suffocating me, and it gave the effect of painted cloth burning...I did not feel well and the nausea increased so much that I ended up vomiting," explained Villas Boas (Ibid.).

Then, matters became decidedly more interesting: according to Villas Boas, his captors left the room, and—"after an immense interval"—in strolled a naked woman. This was no normal woman, however. In his deposition, Villas Boas recorded: "Her hair was fair, almost white, smooth, not very abundant...her eyes were large and blue, more elongated than round, being slanted outwards." He expanded further: "...the cheekbones were very high...her lips were very thin, hardly visible...her body was much more beautiful than that of any woman I have ever known before. It was slim, with high and well-separated breasts, thin waist and small stomach, wide hips and large thighs...another thing that I noted was that her hair in the armpits and in another place was very red, almost the color of blood" (Ibid.).

Perhaps keenly aware that Villas Boas was unsure of what action to take when confronted by a slightly unusual-looking, naked space-girl, the woman elected to take the lead and "came toward me silently, looking at me with the expression of someone wanting something, and she embraced me suddenly and began to rub her head from side to side against my face" (Bowen, 1969). She did indeed want something; and, not surprisingly, Villas Boas was happy to supply it.

...I became uncontrollably excited, sexually, a thing that had never happened to me before," recalled Villas Boas. "I ended up forgetting everything, and I caught hold of the woman, responded to her caresses with other and greater caresses. Finally, she was tired and breathing rapidly. I was still keen, but she was now refusing, trying to escape, to avoid me, to finish with it all." Demonstrating his lack of modesty, Villas Boas opined: "That was what they wanted of me—a good stallion to improve their own stock." And if that statement made Villas Boas's captors sound like animals, well, maybe he had a point. He explained that while the pair got together, "some of the grunts that I heard coming from that woman's mouth at certain moments nearly spoilt everything, giving the disagreeable impression that I was with an animal." This image was further reinforced when, instead of receiving a kiss from the woman, "it ended up with a gentle bite on my chin (Ibid.).
Significantly, Villas Boas claimed that as the woman prepared to leave him,

...she turned to me, pointed at her belly and then pointed toward me and with a smile she finally pointed towards the sky—I think it was in the direction of the south." At that point, Villas Boas's captors returned and gave him a tour of the ship, during which he witnessed "three of the crew...sitting in swivel-chairs, grunting among themselves." While they toiled over their screens and machines, said Villas Boas, he tried to steal a device that was sitting atop a table and that he described as "a square box with a glass lid on it, protecting a dial like the dial of an alarm clock." It was not to be, however: "As quick as lightning one of the men jumped up and, pushing me aside, snatched it from me angrily, and went and put it back in its place (Villas Boas, 1958).

The annoyed crewmen then quickly escorted Villas Boas off their vehicle, after which, from the safety of the field where he had been taken, he watched it ascend into the sky:

> The craft continued to rise slowly into the air until it had reached a height of some 30 to 50 meters…The whirring noise of the air being displaced became much more intense and the revolving dish [that sat atop the object] began to turn at a fearful speed…At that moment, the machine suddenly changed direction, with an abrupt movement, making a louder noise, a sort of 'beat.' Then, listing slightly to one side, that strange machine shot off like a bullet towards the south, at such a speed that it was gone from sight in a few seconds. Then I went back to my tractor. I left the craft at roughly 5:30 in the morning, having entered it at 1:15 in the early hours. So I had been there for four hours and fifteen minutes. A very long time indeed (Bowen, 1969).

The encounter was over and the aliens were forever gone. The young Brazilian farmer ultimately became a respected lawyer, fathering four children—all human. Antonio Villas Boas firmly stood by his strange tale of wild alien sex until his untimely death in 1992 at the age of only 58. And he was not alone in claiming alien contact of the intimate kind.

On February 25, 2009, a legendary figure within the Contactee field— Howard Menger—passed away at his Vero Beach, Florida, home, at the ripe old age of 87. As Greg Bishop notes, Menger was quite a character, and one who had a particular penchant for women of the allegedly non-human variety.

"At the age of 19, Menger enlisted in the Army and saw service in the Pacific during WWII in a flamethrower unit flushing the Japanese out of caves and other hideouts," says Bishop.

> He was wounded and received the Purple Heart. Returning to his native New Jersey in 1946, Menger started a sign painting business and a family. This changed in 1956, when he appeared on the Long John Nebel radio show, along with Contactee George Van Tassel. He talked about contacts with space brothers—and, more specifically, sisters—who appeared to him, beginning when he was 10 years old. Some of his later published descriptions sounded

distinctly sexual in nature, although he carefully couched them in language that could be construed as platonic.

He also started taking pictures of the space people and their ships; although most who saw the photos say that they are quite indistinct. On August 4th of 1956, Menger said he was invited on board one of the flying saucers. The next month he said that the space people took him for a joyride where he saw alien civilizations on other planets and structures on the Moon (Bishop, 2009).

It wasn't long before there was a major development in Menger's life, says Bishop:

Later that year, an attractive young woman named Connie Weber appeared at one of Menger's gatherings. He thought that she was the reincarnation of a blond spacewoman that he had known —in the biblical sense—in a previous life on Venus. He soon left his first wife and family to begin a new life of lectures and touring on the Contactee circuit. *From Outer Space to You*, Menger's 1959 entry into the Contactee fray, made him a regular at Van Tassel's annual spacecraft conventions in Southern California. Connie wrote a book entitled *My Saturnian Lover* about her previous interplanetary relationship with Menger (Ibid.).

In 1960, Menger appeared on a TV show with Nebel and basically recanted his entire story. He later said that he was involved in some sort of Army test of public reaction to possible alien contact. Fortean writer Ivan Sanderson arrived at the Menger residence in the late 1950s and claimed that Menger got very angry with him when Sanderson discovered some equipment and crates in a storage area with 'U. S. Army' stenciled on them (Ibid.).

After this, Menger retired from the public eye and worked on electronic devices he said were designed to harness free-energy and allow mankind to build their own flying saucers. He received no widespread publicity for these inventions. Jim Moseley recalled that Menger attended a UFO convention in the 1970s and 'blew out all the fuses in the hotel' with one of his contraptions (Ibid.).

Bishop concludes: "Despite the claims and controversy, Howard and Connie Menger seemed to be genuinely in love with each other and apparently raised a reasonably happy family. If nothing else, Menger will be remembered as a unique personality who tried to leave a positive message as his legacy" (Ibid.).

11

Aho, Let's Go!

Wayne Aho was a minor cog in the wheel of the Contactees whose little-known claim to cosmic fame has long since passed into obscurity. Nevertheless, his story is not without some significance. A native of Washington State who was born on August 24, 1916, Aho was one of seven children of Finnish homesteaders who worked for most of his adult life as a logger.

Aho claimed to have had his first alien encounter at the age of 12; an event shrouded in mystery and, oddly, barely alluded to by the man himself. It was Aho's alleged extraterrestrial meeting in 1957 that was his crowning glory, however. He grandly asserted that shortly after having attended that year's Giant Rock Interplanetary Space-Craft Convention, he achieved the lofty position of a "Cosmic Master of Wisdom." Like so many of the Contactees whose stories have already been dissected within the pages of this book, Aho maintained that his alien friends who gave him his grand title regularly made their contact with him via telepathy—what else?

So the story went, a group of the now-familiar long-blond-haired extraterrestrials summoned Aho to a desert location, where a George Adamski–type flying saucer zoomed into view; a deep, commanding voice ordered him to spread the words of the Space-Brothers to one and all. Precisely how was Aho expected to inform the world that kindly aliens, who wished us to disarm our nuclear arsenals, were among us? Easy: Aho's cosmic pals enthusiastically urged him to set up his own yearly conference in his home state of Washington. Why the aliens didn't just land and say hello to everyone en masse, instead of having the relatively obscure Aho do all of their hard work for them, was never made clear. Maybe they were lazy. Or mean. Or, worse still: both.

Nevertheless, Aho pressed on undaunted: He enthusiastically flew the flag of the cosmic ones and duly established the Church of the New Age

Wayne Aho, 1950s Contactee. Photo courtesy of Nick Redfern.

in Seattle. Carefully following the instructions of the blonds, Aho held a yearly convention near the entrance to Mount Rainier National Park, in the grandly titled Spacecraft Protective Landing Area for Advancement of Science and Humanities (SPLASH), created in honor of Kenneth Arnold.

In addition to forging ahead with his own gig in Seattle, Aho went on the lecture circuit in California in early 1958 with one Reinhold Schmidt. Everything began very well, and the pair regularly entertained the flying saucer crowd the length and breadth of California—that is, until Schmidt was arrested for, and duly convicted of, grand theft. Like so many of the early Contactees, Schmidt was a real piece of work.

A distinct Johnny-come-lately in the world of the Contactees, Schmidt hailed from Nebraska, where he worked in the grain industry. Born in 1897, he asserted it was on November 5, 1957, that his exposure to the UFO world began. Schmidt was driving through a rural area not far from Kearney, Nebraska, he said, when his attention was drawn to a large cigar-shaped object sitting in the middle of a field.

Schmidt quickly stopped the car and, like so many of the Contactees, was invited aboard the craft by very human-looking aliens—four men and two women who spoke fluent German, no less, and who told Schmidt they hailed from Saturn. Yes, really. There followed a conversation in which the Saturnians expressed their interest in the way in which the Human Race was beginning to venture into space. Very unwisely, Schmidt decided to inform the local police of his alien adventure, who, utterly skeptical, ventured out to the alleged landing site of the huge craft. Unfortunately, the only things they found were Schmidt's footprints, and a mysterious green residue that turned out to be motor oil from a less-than-mysterious can that was located in the trunk of Schmidt's car. There was, however, one more thing: Checks by the police revealed that Schmidt had served time in prison for embezzlement—which was hardly a good indication of his credibility.

Just like practically every other Contactee, Schmidt's 1957 out-of-this-world experience was not a singular event. The aliens, exhibiting infinitely bad judgment, decided that the embezzling Schmidt was worthy of repeat performance after repeat performance. And, the more he learned about the aliens, the weirder things became.

The very human-looking extraterrestrials drank MJB brand coffee. They had on board their spacecraft nothing less than an MG sports-car (or, possibly, a Volkswagen Beetle—the jury is still out on that matter) that they used on Earth whenever they needed to run errands and purchase much-needed groceries. No, I'm really not making this up, but Schmidt very possibly was. But most peculiar of all was the "fact" that the Saturnians' spacecraft was propeller-driven! That odd factor seemingly had no effect on the ability of Schmidt's cosmic friends to traverse the solar system whenever the mood took them, however. Nor did it prevent Schmidt himself from supposedly being taken on an exciting joyride around the Earth.

But, it was when Schmidt elected to move to Bakersfield, California, that matters escalated: Throughout the late 1950s and early 1960s, he became the darling of the little-old-lady brigade that nearly all of the Contactees seemed to attract so effortlessly. It was then that Schmidt's distinctly mean, cruel, and criminal side began to surface again. As well as self-publishing the forgettable *My Contact with the Space People*, Schmidt wowed the wide-eyed septuagenarians and octogenarians that flocked to him in equal heady measures with outlandish tales of cosmic brotherhood. Schmidt also told his eager listeners that during the course of his numerous propeller-driven flights into space, he had succeeded in locating countless valuable mineral deposits—including a unique form of crystal that could cure cancer. Of course, like all true conmen who lack consciences, Schmidt further advised his devoted band of old ladies that he had no money to allow him to begin mining the invaluable crystals, and so would they be kind enough to help him out? Well, of course they were willing to help him out!

Somewhat unbelievably and astonishingly, literally thousands of dollars flowed merrily into the deep pockets of a gleeful Schmidt. By the time the cops busted him, the figure was fast approaching $30,000. Inevitably, arrest and conviction on charges of grand theft quickly followed. After his release from prison some years later, a sheepish Schmidt quietly slunk off back to Nebraska, for the most part thereafter shunning the ufological limelight.

Then there was Wayne Aho's involvement with yet another highly controversial character: Otis T. Carr.

An undoubtedly fascinating character, yet one who was controversial in the absolute extreme, Carr—like Schmidt—first surfaced on the UFO stage during the 1950s. In 1955, Carr founded a company called OTC

Enterprises; with the idea of furthering the work of maverick scientist, Nikola Tesla. How did Carr do this? With the absolute minimum of effort possible, it seems: He merely constructed a small, toy flying saucer—made out of paper—and then had the nerve to claim it was the basis for a "full-size" version that would be capable of flying to, and returning from, the moon in one day, a vehicle he planned to christen OTC X-1.

Carr's ideas may have seemed grand, but they failed to come to fruition. This didn't stop him from making numerous, pseudo-scientific statements about them, however. The OTC X-1, he maintained, used two counter-rotating metal cones, plus spinning electromagnets and capacitors, all powered in turn by a large spinning battery, that would become "activated by the energy of space" (Wikipedia, 2009). No: Saying it slowly doesn't make his Space-Brother-style gobbledygook any more understandable than the first time. If that was not enough, the construction of other fantastic devices was planned by the ambitious Carr, including the "Gravity Electric Generator," "The Utron Electric battery," "The Carrotto Gravity Motor," and the sci-fi-sounding "Photon Gun."

Despite the fact that Carr promised a lot, yet delivered absolutely nothing at all, this didn't stop him from getting a considerable amount of free publicity to promote his wild plans. Ray Palmer's *Fate* magazine welcomed him into the fold like a cosmic combination of a long-lost brother and the prodigal-son returned; and legendary radio host Long John Nebel regularly invited Carr onto his show, throughout which Carr pontificated wildly about his "work." As a perfect, and hilarious, example of this, one night the exchange between Nebel and Carr went as follows:

Nebel: "Can you describe what you're holding in your hand?"

Carr: "This is a dimensional object. It was designed with the dimensions of space itself. We say it is truly the geometric form of space, because it is completely round and completely square" (Wikipedia, 2009).

No one can say that Carr did not entertain Nebel's devoted audience, but whether or not they understood what on earth the man was waffling on about—or how a "dimensional object" could be both round and square—is another matter entirely.

In 1958, Carr struck up a deal with the owner of an amusement park, Frontier City, which was based in Oklahoma City, Oklahoma. According to the terms of the agreement, Carr would construct a 45-foot mock-up version of the OTC X-1, which was to serve as the latest attraction at the amusement park. Of course, nothing of the sort ever happened, and it all ended very badly—for both Carr and Aho.

Initially, however, things seemed to go pretty well. With the deal signed, a delighted Carr, driven by the lure of the almighty dollar and most probably nothing else at all, quickly relocated to Oklahoma City, and asserted to the owners of Frontier City that he was already hard at work on the construction of a 6-foot-diameter prototype of his OTC X-1. The first demonstration, which would see his device rise proudly and majestically into the air to a height of 500 feet, was to take place within the grounds of the park, and in front of the awestruck thousands who had paid good money to get into Frontier City. Everyone was excited for a while.

Carr succeeded in cranking up the excitement level to the absolute max when he told Frontier City that on December 7, 1959, his most ambitious project would come to fruition: On that day, Carr boldly asserted, he planned take to the skies in a finished, working model of the OTC X-1. His destination: the moon! He would not be going alone: right beside him, in the co-pilot's seat, would be none other than Wayne Aho, who had then recently fallen under Carr's hypnotic, car-salesman-like spell.

Like car salesmen everywhere, Carr offered a far more attractive deal than he could ever deliver. Actually, in Carr's case he delivered nothing at all. No meaningful mock-up for the fairground was forthcoming, and neither Carr nor Aho ever made it into space: They didn't even turn up on the historic day in question. Carr had done a runner, leaving a completely bemused Aho wondering where it, and he, had gone wrong. Carr was not destined to stay missing for long, however.

In January 1961, he was arrested, charged, and convicted of "the crime of selling securities without registering the same" in Oklahoma, and received a $5,000 fine—which was reportedly far less than the sums of money he had received from his eager, elderly investors, all of who, were keen to see Carr and Aho soar into space. Worse was to come: Carr no longer had the money to pay the fine, was denied an appeal in March, and ended up in the slammer, where he served a significant part of a 14-year jail term. He died, in quiet obscurity, in Pittsburgh in 1982.

Meanwhile, the gullible Aho, despite being initially charged alongside Carr, was found to be an innocent dupe in Carr's Machiavellian scheme and slunk away with barely a caution. Quite clearly, Aho had been the Igor to Carr's Dr. Frankenstein. Aho continued to skirt around the ufological fringes for the next couple of decades and spent the last years of his life in Gardnerville, Nevada. He died on January 16, 2006, in Carson City, Nevada.

But the story is not quite over. In the wake of Aho's death, Jim Moseley recalled: "We remember when Wayne Aho changed the pronunciation of his name from Aho (long 'a') to Aho ('a' as in father)—presumably because the long 'a' made it sound too much like A-hole" (Moseley, 2006).

There's really nothing that can be added to that.

12

E.T. Infiltration

Robert Dean, a longtime figure within the field of UFO research, maintains that while working with the North Atlantic Treaty Organization (NATO) in the 1960s, he learned that the organization had conducted a secret study of the UFO issue. More controversially, and highly relevant to the subject matter of this book, Dean says that "part of the study stated that [NATO] had come to the conclusion that we had four different civilizations—cultures, intelligences—that were present here on Earth and that were visiting us and interacting with us. One of the most interesting conclusions, and one which struck me most, was that one of the groups—one of the civilizations or cultures that were here on this planet—was identical with us; or rather, that we were identical with them. And that made a vast impression on the people in the investigation" (Dean, 1991).

In 1994, Dean gave a lecture before an audience at the Civic Theater, Leeds, England, during which he elaborated on his knowledge of the human-like aliens said to be present in our environment. Dean revealed that so similar to us was at least one race of extraterrestrial that "they could sit next to you in an airplane or in a restaurant in a coat and tie or a dress and you would never know. They could be sitting next to you in a theater like this" (Dean, 1994).

Most alarming of all, however, were the ramifications that all of the above caused amongst the highest echelons of NATO. "Back in 1964," asserts Dean, "this was a matter of great concern to the admirals and generals at SHAPE Headquarters in Paris. Some of the discussions which went on in the War Room were kind of frightening and some of them were rather amusing. One officer said: 'My God, man, do you realize that these [aliens] could be walking up and down the corridors of SHAPE Headquarters and we wouldn't even know who the hell they were?'" (Ibid.). Robert Dean is not alone in making such claims; and neither are they confined to NATO.

Now in her early-eighties, Marion Shaw worked in the heart of the Pentagon during the 1950s as a secretary with a high-security clearance. While there, she rubbed shoulders with some profoundly significant and well-known figures in the military arena of the day. She also heard tales eerily similar to those told by Robert Dean. According to Shaw, she was allegedly involved in the preparation of several classified reports on "flying saucer stories," one of which referred to deep concerns expressed by the military that very human-appearing aliens had infiltrated certain elements of the U.S. Government. No one seemed quite sure why, however, because there was apparently no concerted effort on the part of the Space-Brothers to subvert or jeopardize the orderly, day-to-day operations of the U.S. infrastructure. Rather, it seemed the aliens were there merely to observe— albeit clandestinely. According to Shaw, the military uncovered the startling truth of the sheer scope of the alien infiltration under truly sensational and surreal circumstances (Shaw, 2009).

In early 1958, Shaw says, the orderly world of a man who she recalls was named Mark Sanford collided violently, literally, and utterly unexpectedly with a race of beings from another world. The location, Shaw asserts, was an area of Louisiana-Texas woods, and the time was late at night. Sanford, Shaw adds, was driving along a perilously narrow lane that was bordered by high, thick bushes and trees that occasionally brushed against the sides of his car as he sped along the winding roads.

As he headed towards his final destination—the Texas town of Kountze—Sanford suddenly became aware of a huge black shadow looming into view at a fantastic speed from the opposite direction. His mind barely had time to take in this startling development when, amid an almighty crash and a sickening groaning of metal, Sanford vaguely felt himself shift alarmingly to the left at a fantastic rate.

In the next instant, Sanford was suddenly upside down, then upright, then once more upside down. He caught a brief glimpse of the moon, then darkness, then the light of the Earth's satellite once again. Even amid the overriding confusion, Sanford knew precisely what was happening: His car had been hit by another vehicle, had been pushed down a slight bank, and was flipping over, time and again. Mentally, he tried to brace himself for the moment when the vehicle came to a crashing and bone-crunching halt.

Sanford had no idea how long he lay in the twisted wreckage of his once-immaculate car. It seemed like forever, but it was probably no more than two or three minutes. Dulled and confused, he crawled out of the twisted remains of his vehicle. Trying to get his bearings, Sanford just about managed to raise himself to an upright position, at which point he could not fail to notice that near the shattered remains of his own vehicle was a large black car sitting on its crushed roof. Inch by inch, Sanford made his way towards the vehicle that had created the carnage in which he now found himself directly immersed.

As Sanford limped toward the car, the moon cast its light on a shocking scene: Sprawled around the vehicle were four "very tall men in suits," one of whom was "shocked and sitting with his elbows on his knees," while the remaining three were clearly dead—their bodies and limbs horribly distorted and broken by the trauma of the crash. All four sported heads of long, thick, blond hair—very atypical of the average mid-1950s American male, of course. Suddenly, out of the darkness, and emanating from the direction of the road, Sanford could hear the sounds of men shouting. He turned his head in their direction and could see a military truck parked at the edge of the road, from which a small group of uniformed personnel had already disgorged, and who were quickly making their way to the crash site.

Even in his disoriented state, Sanford was reportedly appalled by the sight of one of the soldiers "smacking" the lone survivor across his face with a glove; something which—Shaw says—"will always stay with me, after I typed Mr. Sanford's interview. Why they had to do that, I still don't know now. The man was scared and his friends were dead. He hadn't hurt us. Probably it was a bit of arrogance, and we wanted to show him some force. They took him and his friends' bodies away, and Mr. Sanford gave his first interview at Fort Hood [Texas]."

Shaw expands that the military presence was no coincidence: They had been clandestinely trailing the vehicle for several days, having been ordered to do so by the "flying saucer project people," who "had been trying to catch one of these men since before Mr. Adamski's book, and finally got four at one time." Shaw claims not to know much more, aside from hearing rumors that (a) the three recovered bodies were "autopsied very lengthy [sic];" (b) the "surviving man" was harshly interrogated ("but gave up nothing, but he wasn't here to hurt us"), and lived in quarantine "for the longest time and finally became friendly," (c) that "Mr. Sanford was paid to be quiet, and did;" and (d) the ownership of the "alien car" was traced to none other than a source in the Pentagon who—it was somehow learned—had secretly met with his blond friends on several occasions to discuss "atomic things," and who later "disappeared in Belize, it was said" (Shaw, 2009).

Marion Shaw's story is, of course, truly outlandish: Tales of long-haired extraterrestrials clandestinely traveling the country—not in flying saucers, but in big black cars; claims of concerned Pentagon staff dispatching teams of alien-hunters to ruthlessly chase down those same extraterrestrials; and rumors of secret collaboration between the Space-Brothers and elements of the official world collectively sound like the stuff of wild science fiction. But does that mean we should dismiss Shaw's story as merely the odd ravings of an old lady with equally old memories? Possibly not: Tales of the bodies of tall, long-haired aliens of a distinctly Space-Brother variety having been secretly autopsied by the U.S. military most assuredly do not begin and end with Marion Shaw.

The late Leonard Stringfield, who was one of the world's leading collectors of stories on the subject of "UFO crash-retrievals," learned in 1981 from a certain French professor that at Wright-Patterson Air Force Base, Dayton, Ohio, the mangled bodies of at least two very human-like extraterrestrials were said to be held, following their alleged recovery from a presumed UFO crash or accident:

They were very tall…and bore hideous mutilations on their bodies, *as if they had been the victims of a road accident* [Note from the author: emphasis mine]. The heads of these two creatures were intact. The forehead [was] high and broad. [They had] very long blond hair. The eyes were stretched towards the temples which gave them an Asiatic look. The nose and mouth were small. The lips were thin, perfectly delineated. The chin was small and slightly pointed. The two faces were beardless. Despite slight differences in their facial appearances, the two humanoids looked like twins (Stringfield, 1982).

No study of claims of aliens infiltrating the Pentagon would be complete without mention of the 1950s claims of the late Frank Stranges, founder and former president of the National Investigations Committee on UFOs; and president of the International Evangelical Crusades, and the International Theological Seminary of California.

Greg Bishop says: "Stranges most lasting legacy may be his narrative in [his book] *Stranger at the Pentagon*, the story of Venusian Captain 'Valiant Thor.' According to Stranges, after Val had met with the president and members of the Joint Chiefs [allegedly in the Pentagon on March 16, 1957], he had a meeting with Stranges at the Pentagon. Val Thor sounded (and looked) like Michael Rennie's portrayal of the ufonaut Klaatu in *The Day the Earth Stood Still*" (Bishop, 2008).

Stranges recalled: "Being a minister of the Gospel of Jesus Christ, as well as a student of the Bible for many years, coupled with my experience as an special investigator, I felt as though my senses were functioning properly and that I knew exactly what I was about to do. I was on my guard for fakes and frauds. In walked a man, about six feet tall, perhaps 185 pounds, brown wavy hair, brown eyes. His complexion appeared normal and slightly tanned. As I approached him, and he looked at me, it was as though he looked straight through me. With a warm smile and extending his hand, he greeted me by name. His genuineness astonished me, but quickly I understood. As I gripped his hand, I was somewhat surprised to feel the soft texture of his skin… like that of a baby but with the strength of a man that silently testified to his power and intensity" (Stranges, 1967).

Have human-like aliens infiltrated the Pentagon? Photo courtesy of the Department of Defense.

Stranges elaborated:

He told me that his purpose in coming was to help mankind return to the Lord. He spoke in positive terms...always with a smile on his face. He said that man was further away from God than ever before, but there was still a good chance if man looks in the right place. He told me he had been here nearly three years and would depart in just a few months.

Claiming that he would not use force to speak with men in authority in America, he was happy to consult with them at their invitation. He further stated that thus far only a few men in Washington knew of his existence in the Pentagon. And few leaders had availed themselves of his advice during these past three years.

He felt there was still so much to do and yet his time of departure was getting near. He told me that Jesus Christ would not force men to be saved from their mistakes, even though He had already made a way for mankind to be redeemed through His shed blood. When I asked him where he was from, he replied, 'I am from the Planet that is called Venus.'

I asked him how many visitors from Venus were presently on Earth and he said, 'There are presently 77 of us walking among you in the United States. We are constantly coming and going'" (Ibid.)

And if the story of Marion Shaw can be believed, those same aliens were also fatally crashing their cars, while simultaneously fleeing bands of E.T.-hunting soldiers.

We may never know for sure if Frank Stranges, tales were true or not; but the final word on this matter goes to Greg Bishop: "Other Contactees met their space brothers in deserts, along deserted highways, and in coffee shops. Frank Stranges met Val Thor in the hallowed halls of military power, making him the only Contactee to be able to claim the imprimatur of officialdom' (Bishop, 2008).

13

Aliens on the Mountain

Brown Mountain is a low-lying ridge, 2,600 feet high, approx. 1 1/2 miles in length, and situated in the Pisgah National Forest near Morganton, North Carolina. Its eastern ridge forms part of the boundary between Burke and Caldwell counties, and is composed of Cranberry Granite; a rock which also underlies countless square miles of the north-side of North Carolina's famous Blue Ridge Mountains.

But Brown Mountain is no normal mountain.

For centuries it has been home to ghostly, unidentified aerial intruders: glowing balls of light that fly around the area late at night, gliding through the trees, and provoking interest, intrigue, fear, and amazement in those that encounter them. Moreover, the Brown Mountain Lights— as they have become known—may very well be inextricably linked with the controversy of the Contactees.

Not surprisingly, the mysterious lights have become deeply ingrained in the folklore of the people of North Carolina—and for centuries, no less. Native American Indian folklore dating back to around 1200 describes a fierce battle between Cherokee and Catawba warriors, and maintains that the lights represent the spirits of the wives of those same warriors, doomed to forever search for their slain loved ones by night. A second, and somewhat similar, legend tells of a man hunting on the mountain, who became lost and whose slave came looking for him—armed with a lantern. So the story goes: The Brown Mountain Lights can be explained as the now-spectral slave, still searching in vain for his master.

Then, there is the folkloric tale that surfaced in 1850, and that told of a pregnant woman in the area who disappeared amid rumors that she had been murdered by her husband, who had fallen for another woman in the area. Those on the mountain who saw the lights while searching for the woman's body, it was claimed, were actually seeing the murdered woman's amorphous spirit. Believing this, the guilt-stricken husband confessed to the murder, but fled town before he could be arrested—or so the story goes.

Not everyone was convinced that the lights were in any way anomalous, however. In 1771, a German engineer named Gerard Will de Brahm offered a far-less-provocative theory: "The Mountain emits nitrous vapors which are borne by the wind; and when laden winds meet each other the niter inflames, sulphurates [sic], and deteriorates" (Wikipedia, 2009).

A different, but no less down-to-earth, explanation was provided in October 1913. At the request of Representative E.Y. Webb of North Carolina, a member of the U.S. Geological Survey—one D.B. Sterrett—was dispatched to Brown Mountain in an attempt to try to determine the origin of the lights. Sterrett suggested that those who reported seeing the lights were actually viewing the headlights of locomotives traveling through the Catawba Valley, which is located south of Brown Mountain. However, Sterrett's theory was thrown into doubt when, three years later, the valley was flooded, bridges were damaged, and the trains were unable to run until significant repairs and rebuilding were undertaken. During the period in which the trains were out of action, the mysterious lights were still regularly seen.

The U.S. Geological Survey was not finished with the lights, however. In 1922, a detailed, *X-Files*-style official report—titled *Origin of the Brown Mountain Light in North Carolina*—was prepared by an employee of the agency named George Rogers Mansfield. Interestingly, the Fox Mulder–like Mansfield spent a lot of time personally investigating the reports of the strange lights: He scoured the area for two weeks in March and April 1922, and, on four occasions, even got to see the lights. Mansfield was not convinced their presence was evidence of unexplained phenomena, however. In the concluding section of his report, he wrote: "About 47 percent of the lights that the writer was able to study instrumentally were due to automobile headlights, 33 percent to locomotive headlights, 10 percent to stationary lights, and 10 percent to brush fires" (Mansfield, 1922).

Despite the findings of the U.S. Geological Survey, there were those who were adamant that the Brown Mountain Lights could not be explained away quite so easily. One of those was a local man named Ralph L. Lael, who was the author of a curious, little self-published booklet that surfaced in 1965, titled, unsurprisingly, *The Brown Mountain Lights*. Lael claimed a truly extraordinary and definitive Contactee-style encounter on the mountain, in which the lights played an integral role.

Lael was quite a character: Born in 1909, he ran for Congress in 1948 (while giving a political speech in Hickory, North Carolina, he was pelted with eggs) and was the proud owner of the notably named Outer Space Rock Shop Museum—more about that shortly. Lael's booklet has been overlooked by many students of the Contactee issue, and yet it is one that potentially sheds much-welcome light upon what may be at the heart of the puzzle. By Lael's own admission, he first heard about the lights in 1922—from his father, who had personally seen "great balls of fire rising and bursting above the top of the mountain." Writing in the present tense in his booklet, Lael said: "My plan is to go to the source of the lights and see if I can come in contact with them at night" (Lael, 1965). According to Lael, that is precisely what he did, at a location on the mountain where the lights had reportedly been seen on numerous occasions.

Aside from occurring at a vague point in the late 1950s, the date of Lael's initial claimed encounter is unknown—but that does not detract from its significance. As Lael told it, he witnessed a number of unidentified lights while "on top of Wild Cat Knob" (Ibid.) Interestingly, Lael recorded in his booklet that as several unidentified aerial lights began to appear before his eyes, they seemed to react to his presence. Ten to 12 feet across, and with three "feeler's" protruding from it, one such light approached him, "as if it was alive and had intelligence" (Ibid.). Both it and the other lights then seemed to melt back into the surface of Wild Cat Knob, and a distinctly shaky Lael headed for the safety of his home, on Highway 101, approximately 2 miles from the foot of Brown Mountain. But that encounter was nothing compared with what reportedly occurred in 1962, during the course of a further experience.

Linda Wolff, whose father's uncle was Lael himself, says:

…the lights communicated with him and beckoned him to follow them to a large rock. As he stood at the rock, a door appeared and he stepped in. Once inside, he turned to look back at the door and it was no longer there.

Looking forward once again, the rock appeared to go under the mountain without end. The walls were of solid crystal and voice communication began from what we, in these times, would term an alien. The alien explained why Earth was chosen to be observed and how life on our planet once was. He told about the future of our planet if man does not change his ways. He then said what we call 'space ships' are really vessels used by aliens from the planet Venus to patrol the Universe" (Wolff, 2004).

Timothy Green Beckley, author, researcher and publisher, met Lael in 1969, and, at the time, recorded what allegedly happened next:

Lael…was offered a ride to Venus—which he accepted. Arriving two days later on Earth's sister planet he was introduced to men who were said to have been direct descendents of the people from the planet Pewam [according to Lael's alien informants, all that remains of Pewam today is that which we call the Asteroid Belt]. One is a rather attractive woman named Noma who is quite beautifully dressed in a bra and panties set. While on Venus Lael is shown what appear to be newsreels of the destruction of Pewam as well as scenes going on back on Earth (Beckley, 1969).

Another individual introduced to Lael was "Heath," described as being "about 40 years old, [and] 6 feet 9 inches tall" (Ibid). Perhaps of significance is Lael's claim that, at one point, Heath turned on a large television-style device that provided real-time imagery of a discussion in the U.S. Senate on the then-escalating Cuban Missile Crisis.

It was this particular discussion that prompted Heath to inform Lael that the warming up in the Cold War was similar to that which led to the destruction of the planet Pewam. Heath explained that the population of Pewam was divided into two sections ("Eastern World and Western World") that, after growing tension, went to war, and, in doing so, utterly destroyed their world in a fiery, destructive inferno. The survivors, Heath added, fled their home-world, before being accepted by the "light people" of Venus, on whose planet they had resided "for the last six thousand years" (Lael, 1965).

Heath explained to Lael that, as Pewam shattered into myriad fragments, a number of those same fragments headed towards the Earth, raining down death and destruction in the process. Heath also told Lael that a "great boat" was being built (by a man named "Noa") in anticipation of the chaos that would surely erupt when the rocky pieces of Pewam collided with the Earth. Somewhat controversially, Heath claimed that those who directed Noa to build his "great boat" were "people banished from Pewam for different crimes committed on Pewam. Most of them were political prisoners" (Ibid.).

Heath continued: "You have a book on Earth that gives a record of this great disaster[;] it is only part of the truth. Noa was afraid to give the whole truth to the following generations. But the time has come that the people on Earth should know the truth, so it is possible they may be spared destruction." Lael was then allegedly shown graphic imagery of the great flood as described in the pages of *The Bible*, and was told that humankind needed to change its ways—unless it wished to be destroyed by the "Light People of Venus" (Ibid.).

Somewhat curiously, Lael suddenly ended his story there, with an enigmatic explanation: "There are many things I have seen and heard that I cannot reveal here because of my obligations to the Brown Mountain Lights" (Ibid.).

But the controversial story is not finished.

Micah Hanks, a veritable sleuth when it comes to paranormal investigations, and who lives deep in the heart of North Carolina, has

Micah Hanks, researcher of the mysterious Brown Mountain Lights. Photo courtesy of Micah Hanks.

studied another aspect of the curious life of Ralph Lael: "Aside from Lael's incredible testimony regarding contact with foreigners from planet Pewam, he had what was arguably his most intriguing artifact on display to the public [in his shop]: an 'alien mummy.' Little is known about exactly what the small mummified body may have been, though as far as I have been able to tell, there have been some reports over the years that involved Lael telling folks who had lived in the Linville/Morganton area that it 'might have been a pygmy' of some sort."

He continues:

> Dr. Chris Blake, a writer and researcher who lives in the area today, discussed this with me during a *MUFON* [*Mutual UFO Network*] experiment we attended that involved mapping a portion

of the Lineville wilderness where the area's famous ghost lights are seen, and alluded that many locals thought it might have been a sideshow attraction that Lael had purchased or had been given.

Apparently, after Lael passed away his shop was demolished, leading some to believe that it and the alien body within were intentionally destroyed in some effort to cover up the fact that it might have been a bona fide extraterrestrial. But perhaps the body was never destroyed at all.

Hanks asks:

Could it be that the demolition of Lael's shop had actually been intended to cause speculation as to what had really happened to Lael's prize possession, and that the mummy itself was spirited away to some undisclosed location? Or even more likely, was the item merely thrown away with other of Lael's belongings, since the building was being prepared for destruction anyway?

Regardless of the ultimate answers to those questions, Hanks believes that Lael's "alien mummy" was probably the handiwork of a "famous creator of curiosities named Homer Tate" (Hanks, 2008).

Tate was an interesting figure, to say the least. Born in 1884 in Poetry, Texas, to a resolutely Mormon family, he worked variously as a farmer, miner, gas-station owner, and even town-sheriff. In 1945 he moved to live in Apache Junction, Arizona, where he began to create and sculpt all manner of weird, little creatures. Doug Higley—a skilled craftsman whose very own monstrous creations can be seen in museums and sideshows across the world—says that Tate's "little 'Pygmy' bodies and crudely crafted Mummies and 'Freaks'" were created "for the sole purpose of humbugging a nation," and "would be shown coast to coast in Roadside Museums and Circus Sideshows" (Higley, 2005).

Tate's granddaughter, Vada, has added some welcome data, too, with respect to the way in which Tate made his little monsters: "I know he scoured the desert when he lived at Apache Junction for animal skin and bones, but I also know he used human hair from any source he could find…he was pretty resourceful" (Ibid.).

According to Higley matters came to a halt when Tate "got in a bit of trouble," and his son, Martin, sold off the entire beastly collection (Ibid.).

Higley adds: "Homer Tate's 'Pygmy' shenanigans hadn't gone over well with the rest of the upright Mormon Tates" (Ibid.).

In all probability, one of Tate's constructs ultimately found its way to Ralph Lael's store, and the legend of the "alien mummy" began in earnest. Even though Lael's prized possession had far less exotic origins than many wanted to believe, we should not entirely discount the notion that something very real and profound happened to Lael on that lonely night atop Brown Mountain in 1962, and while the world teetered precariously on the brink of catastrophic nuclear destruction.

14

"Believe in us, but not too much."

On April 24, 1964, one of the most credible UFO cases on record occurred. The witness was a highly reliable one: Lonnie Zamora, a sergeant with the Socorro, New Mexico, Police Department. Less well known, however, is that the Socorro event was preceded that same day by a very similar incident that bore all the hallmarks of a classic encounter of the Contactee kind. But, first: a bit of background on the Socorro affair.

At approximately 5:45 p.m. on the day at issue, 31-year-old Zamora was pursuing a car which was flouting the speed-limit on U.S. Highway 85. While still in pursuit, Zamora was startled by a loud roar and a brilliant blue "cone of flame" that emanated from an area to the southwest, some 2,400 feet away. Realizing this was not an everyday occurrence, Zamora broke off chasing the speeding vehicle and drove his patrol car in the direction from which the flames and roar surfaced. In order to reach the area, Zamora was obliged to travel along a little-used road which passed over a number of hills and gullies.

After two or three attempts to drive his car up a gravel-covered incline, Zamora finally reached a crest, got out of his vehicle, and was astonished by the sight that confronted him. Sitting on girder-like legs was a strange "egg-shaped" object unlike anything Zamora had ever seen before. But that was not all: "I saw two small figures in what resembled white coveralls, pretty close to the object on its northwest side, as if inspecting it…One of the figures seemed to turn as if it heard or saw my car coming. It must have seen me, 'cause when it turned and looked straight at my car, it seemed startled—almost seemed to jump somewhat'" (Sanford, 1966). This proved too much for Zamora, who was totally unprepared for the encounter.

A CIA document on the case takes up the story from there:

Thinking that the object was going to explode [Zamora] became frightened. He turned, ran back to get behind the police car, bumping his leg and losing his glasses on the way. He crouched down, shielding his eyes with his arm while the noise continued for another ten seconds. At this time the noise stopped and he looked up. The object had risen to a point about 15 to 20 feet above the ground and the flame and smoke had ceased to come from the object…The object had a red marking about 1 foot or maybe 16 inches in height, shaped like a crescent with a vertical arrow and horizontal line underneath.

The object hovered in this spot for several seconds and then flew off in a SW direction following the contour of the gully. It cleared the dynamite shack by not more than 3 feet. He watched the object disappear in the distance over a point on Highway 85 about 6 miles from where he was standing. The object took about 3 minutes to travel that far. Disappearance was by fading in the distance and at no time did he observe the object to rise more than 20 feet off the ground (CIA, 1966).

Zamora was not the only one to be surprised that day by what may very well have been the same craft and crew. For the details, we have to turn to long-time Fortean authority, Patrick Huyghe, who outlines the facts:

At 10 a.m. on April 24, 1964—about 10 hours before the Socorro event—Gary Wilcox, a farmer living in Tioga City, New York, saw a craft that very much resembles the one seen in Socorro, as well as two small figures who were dressed almost identically.

Wilcox described seeing a shiny object in the woods. As he approached it, he saw a 20-foot-long, egg-shaped object hovering about 2 feet above the ground. When Wilcox began to examine the object, he was confronted by two beings, each about four feet tall and wearing silvery white outfits that covered their heads. The stocky figures were carrying trays of soil.

One of the beings approached Wilcox and began talking to him in English. They spoke for two hours about such subjects as air pollution, space probes, agricultural methods, and the fact that the beings claimed to be from Mars. The Martians told Wilcox not to tell anyone about his experience, then entered their ship, which emitted an idling sound as it took off (Huyghe, 2001).

Of course, Wilcox's account—of the aliens expressing concerns about pollution, and identifying their point of origin as the planet Mars—was definitively Contactee-driven, whereas Zamora's experience revolved around a close encounter with an unidentified vehicle. That does not, however, exclude the possibility of a direct connection between these two thought-provoking events.

An intriguing 1960s case that has undoubted Contactee overtones to it, can be found in the now-declassified UFO files of the FBI. Dating from October 10, 1967, the report—prepared by a special-agent of the FBI—reads as follows:

A young white female, who refused to give her name, appeared at the Dallas [Texas] FBI Office on October 9, 1967. She stated she is interested in Unidentified Flying Objects (UFOs) and has received a quantity of information concerning beings from outer space. She stated she will not reveal her identity as she would feel like a fool if the information is not true. She stated if it is true, however, she will meet with interested officials and furnish all the information she has, provided nothing is done to endanger her safety.

She stated in July 1967, she met a being from another planet who had assumed Earthly form. He gave her certain information, then he was picked up and departed from the Earth on August 21, 1967. She stated she then received messages from non-Earthly sources in a manner she refused to discuss. She stated these sources told her of the following:

1. An anti-missile missile was fired at a UFO over Africa on May 22, 1962, but the UFO was protected by its 'force field.'

2. A UFO was detected 22,000 miles from Earth by radar about August 6, 1967.

3. A UFO was detected over Antarctica August 20, 1967.

4. A UFO was detected over the 'Dewline' in the past week and was shot down, and beings from outer space are trying to recover it.

Informant would furnish no further details. She stated if this information is true, she will know other information she received is true, and will furnish full details. This will include information regarding the destruction of a moon explorer vehicle by beings from outer space, and how those beings shot down the Russian Cosmonaut.

She stated she fears for her life if it becomes known she contacted officials, as persons who saw UFOs have died mysteriously in the past. She stated if Air Force officials want to contact her she can be reached by a message to a telephone number she has given an FBI agent, and she will meet officials at the Dallas FBI Office only (FBI, 1967).

There is no doubt that this case is rich in Contactee-like data. For example, there is the reference to the woman having "received a quantity of information concerning beings from outer space." She advised the FBI that contact had been made with "a being from another planet who had assumed Earthly form." And, subsequent to the departure of the alien, she had been the recipient of "messages from non-Earthly sources" that had come to her attention via "a manner she refused to discuss."

Unfortunately, a one-page memorandum referring the above details to the Air Force Office of Special Investigations aside, Dallas FBI records reflect no further contact with the woman at issue. Yet, her claims are not so easy to brush aside as the mere ravings of a deluded soul.

Less than two weeks after the woman visited the Dallas Office of the FBI, the former Soviet Union instigated a semi-official research project aimed at resolving the UFO problem. According to the Soviets, the project had been proposed in the wake of five, then-recent, well-authenticated UFO sightings. Of course, one might suggest that this was mere coincidence, and had no bearing upon the young woman's claims of significant UFO events—also in 1967. However, of equal interest is the fact that only two months later, one of the most sensational of all UFO contact cases occurred—as Greg Bishop reveals.

"Early on the morning of December 3rd, 1967, patrolman Herbert Schirmer was making his rounds near Ashland, Nebraska. He saw what he thought was a truck disabled near the side of the road. As he neared the object and switched on his high-beams, Schirmer realized that it was no truck. An oval object with red lights shining from inside was hovering about eight feet from the ground. As Schirmer watched, the thing began to ascend, shooting flames accompanied by a 'siren-like' sound. It passed a few feet

Greg Bishop, a leading authority on the Contactee movement. Courtesy of Nick Redfern.

over the patrol car and was lost from sight in a few seconds.

"The incident seemed to last about 10 minutes, but when Schirmer returned to the police station to write up his report, he found that he could not account for almost an hour of time. His entry in the logbook simply stated 'Saw a flying saucer at the junction of highways 6 and 63, believe it or not!'

[Schirmer] was brought to Boulder, Colorado to undergo regressive hypnosis with psychologist Dr. Leo Sprinkle. During the session, it was revealed that after he first came upon the UFO, Schirmer had been approached by three human-looking beings between 4.5 and 5 feet in height. He later drew a picture of the one he took to be the 'leader.' The being addressed him, asking 'Are you the watchman of this place?' Schirmer said 'Sure,' and after assurances that he wouldn't shoot at the ship, they took him on a short tour of the interior. The Ufonauts all wore tight-fitting uniforms with fabric that covered their heads. On the right breast of their clothing, there was a patch or embroidery depicting a winged serpent.

Schirmer was later promoted to chief of police for Ashland, but had to quit after personal, psychological and marital problems ruined his concentration. He was haunted by the experience for years afterwards."

Bishop concludes with an interesting observation: "The thing that makes this case a significant one for me is [that] during the course of the regressions, Schirmer said that the one being he talked to left him with this admonition: 'We want you to believe in us, 'but not too much' (Bishop, 2008).

Was this enigmatic statement an indication that human-like aliens were indeed trying to get some form of message across to the human race, but were concerned about announcing their presence on a planet-wide scale, and, consequently, preferred to do so at a restricted level, and only to small bodies of people in isolated settings? Sadly, more than four decades on, we may never really know.

15

Saucers in the '70s

During the early hours of October 28, 1973, Dionisio Llanca, a truck-driver, was negotiating Highway 3 near Bahia Blanca—a city located south-west of the province of Buenos Aires, Argentina—when he was forced to stop his vehicle, which for several hours had been suffering from a slow puncture. As he began to jack up the wheel, Llanca was enveloped in a yellow beam of light that emanated from a flying saucer-shaped object hovering 15 to 20 feet from the ground. Semi-paralyzed by the light beam, Llanca was amazed to see behind him three humanoids, all staring intently in his direction.

The two men and one woman were each about 5-foot-6 in height and wore tight-fitting, grey, one-piece outfits and three-quarter length boots. Again, they looked very human and had long blond hair. Suddenly, Llanca was forcibly grabbed, and a device was placed on the index finger of his left hand. He then became disorientated and fainted. Later, Llanca recalled the beings had informed him they had been present on Earth since 1950 and offered the following warning: "[Your] planet is bound to suffer very grave catastrophes if [your] behavior continues as it is at present" (*Flying Saucer Review*, 1974).

The peace-loving hippies from beyond the veil had left their calling card yet again.

Two months after the experience of Dionisio Llanca, a Frenchman named Claude Maurice Marcel Vorilhon underwent an experience of a distinctly Contactee-style nature that eventually elevated him to truly stratospheric levels and that today, shows no signs of abating.

Born on September 30, 1946, in Vichy, France, Vorilhon was raised in Ambert, attended a Catholic boarding-school until the age of 15, at which point he left and hitchhiked to Paris—where he spent several years playing music: on the streets, and in cafes and cabarets. Vorilhon's persistence and enthusiasm paid off: It was during this period that he met one Lucien Morisse, who was the director of a national radio show in France. Morisse was on the look-out for new talent, and recognized that Vorilhon had the potential to be a star. As a result, the young Vorilhon was offered a recording contract, adopted the name of Claude Celler, and released six singles—one of which, "Honey and Cinnamon," became a minor hit. Unfortunately, everything came to a tragic halt in September 1970, when Morisse committed suicide, leaving Vorilhon wondering what to do next.

Fascinated by the worlds of sports cars and motor-racing, Vorilhon decided to move away from music. He established a magazine he named *Autopop*—the first issue of which was published in May 1971—allowed him to indulge in his passion for test-driving new and cool-looking cars. But fate had yet another path in store for Vorilhon, and it had absolutely nothing to do with automobiles or the music industry: Alien entities from a far-away world were about to radically alter his life.

Like so many of the earlier Contactees, Vorilhon's initial encounter occurred at an isolated location: in his case it was an old, inactive volcano situated at Puy de Lasollas, near the capital of Avergne, to which he felt inexplicably compelled to drive on the day in question, December 13, 1973.

Researcher Jacques Vallee says: "The weather was foggy, overcast. He suddenly saw a blinking red light, and something like a helicopter came down and hovered two yards above the ground. It was the size of a small bus, conical on top…A stairway appeared, and a child-like occupant came out, smiling with a glow around his body" (Vallee, 2008).

As was the case with just about all the Contactees from George Adamski onward, the alien occupant—whose name was Yahweh—had both a message and a task for the amazed Vorilhon. Both became abundantly clear over the course of the next week, during which time further clandestine meetings with the alien entity supposedly occurred—the details of which Vorilhon collectively described within *Le Livre qui dit la Vérité* (*The Book Which Tells the Truth*), which made the claim that highly evolved scientists from another planet—operating with the benefit of 25,000 years of supremely advanced technology—were responsible for the creation of life on Earth, which was achieved via expert DNA manipulation.

So Vorilhon says he was told, the scientists in question were originally known as the Elohim ("those who came from the sky"), and that during the formative years of human civilization, they dispatched no less than 40 "prophets" (including Moses, Jesus and Buddha) to Earth as part of a concerted effort to get their message of love and peace across—something that was not entirely successful due to the fact that the overwhelming primitive nature of human society at the time resulted in the Elohim's messages becoming wildly distorted and misinterpreted. But all was not lost: Enter the task that was about to befall the man once known as Claude Celler.

Vorilhon claimed he was given the lofty mission of telling the world of humanity's ancient origins in anticipation of the day when the aliens would finally return en masse. Not only that: Vorilhon's extraterrestrial emissary told him he had been chosen to build for them a "residential embassy," and that he should establish a movement to be called MADECH, which stood for "Movement pour l'accueil des Elohim createurs de l'humanite," or, in English, "Movement for welcoming the Elohim, creators of humanity." The other-worldly operation had begun in earnest.

On September 19, 1974, Vorilhon held his first public conference in Paris where at least some of the story was told, and which attracted an impressively sized audience of more than two-thousand. Formal establishment of MADECH soon followed. As time progressed, Claude Morris Marcel Vorilhon became known only as Raël, and MADECH became the International Raëlian Movement—which steadily grew from strength to strength, and on a truly global scale, too.

Without doubt, however, the most controversial, newsworthy, and talked-about development came in the latter part of 2002. On December 26th, Brigitte Boisselier, a Raëlian Bishop and CEO of a biotechnology company called Clonaid, announced the birth of a baby called Eve—who was described as being nothing less than a human clone. Inevitably, a veritable furor erupted amid concerns relative to ethical issues, legal matters, religion, claims of hoaxing, and more. The Raëlians, however, were utterly unmoved by what ultimately turned out to be a wealth of predominantly negative attention. Spokespeople for the movement suggested that the birth of Eve was just the first step on the road to achieving an infinitely more important goal: Accelerated growth processes, combined with mind-transfer and cloning, said the Raëlians, offered the world the very real possibility of eternal life.

The Raëlians have good reason for wanting to try to achieve some form of everlasting existence in the physical realm: Their firm belief is that the extraterrestrial Elohim were solely responsible for the creation of the human race; and, as a result of that same belief, they deny the existence of a god or gods, or a soul that survives bodily death. In other words, from the perspective of the Raëlians, cloning may well be the only means by which we can ever hope to attain neverending lives. It seems that many people agree with the Raëlians: Estimates suggest that membership figures of the organization are nearing six-figures.

Not everyone who came into contact with the UFO puzzle in the 1970s was as lucky as Raël, however. Indeed, one particularly notorious affair proved to be downright tragic—as will now become apparent.

Marshall Herff Applewhite, Jr. entered this world on May 17, 1931, in Spur, Texas, to parents Louise Haecker and Marshall Herff Applewhite, Sr. The elder Marshall was a Presbyterian minister whose wish was that his son would follow in his footsteps. It didn't quite work out that way, however. After graduating from high-school in 1954, Applewhite entered the Army, and received postings to Salzburg, Austria, and White Sands, New Mexico, where he received an assignment as a Signal Corps instructor.

After an honorable discharge from the military, Applewhite took a position as a music teacher at a Texas-based college; then gravitated to the stage, taking on lead roles in musicals in both the Lone Star State and Colorado. He eventually achieved the position of Choir Director at the

Houston-based St. Mark's Episcopal Church, sung with the Houston Grand Opera, and taught music at the University of St. Thomas—also in Houston. But it was not all good news, however. As evidence that things were not at all well within the mind of Applewhite, in 1970 he was fired from his job at the University of St. Thomas. The reason for his dismissal was somewhat tactfully described as being due to "health problems of an emotional nature."

In 1972, Applewhite's life changed radically: Still only in his early 40s, he suffered a heart-attack. While he was recovering (at a Houston, Texas, psychiatric hospital, no less) Applewhite met a nurse named Bonnie Nettles. Not long after, the two began dating. And it also wasn't long before the pair was embroiled in deep controversy.

On August 28, 1974, Applewhite was busted by the cops in Harlingen, Texas, for stealing credit cards. That was okay, though: After Nettles told him that he possessed special astrological attributes, Applewhite shrugged off his encounters with the police and declared himself "the individual in whose mind was held that of Christ, the reincarnation of Jesus Christ" (Wikipedia). Some 12 months later, the pair succeeded in establishing a group called Total Overcomers Anonymous (which ultimately became the infamous Heaven's Gate cult), toured the United States speaking at length on matters pertaining to advanced alien entities, and traveled to far-off worlds and amazing dimensions—the usual fodder, in other words.

Also in 1975, Applewhite and Nettles convinced no less than 20 people from Waldport, Oregon, to join their group. Applewhite enticed them into doing so by assuring the eager disciples that extraterrestrial beings would soon put in an amazing and life-changing appearance for the chosen ones. But chosen or not, not a single one of the group was blessed with an alien visitation. Disgusted and disheartened, many of the Waldport crew departed for pastures new; however, they were soon replaced, and before long membership of the group were fast approaching three-figures—many of whom followed the dynamic duo as they toured the country, spreading the other-worldly word.

For much of the late 1970s and 1980s, Nettles and Applewhite stayed under the ufological radar—largely because not that many people of any real standing within the UFO arena particularly cared about them, their beliefs, or their activities. But that situation was destined to change—for the worse. After Nettles died from the effects of cancer in 1985, Applewhite became ever-more unstable and even underwent a surgical castration. Ouch.

But it was in 1997 that matters came to a head. On March 19th of that year, Applewhite taped himself speaking of mass suicide, and asserted that such action was the only way to evacuate the Earth. For the most part, the members of the Heaven's Gate cult were utterly against suicide, but, both controlled and manipulated by Applewhite's charisma, they came to accept his words. Indeed, convincing his then-38 followers that nothing less than an extraterrestrial space vehicle was trailing the comet Hale-Bopp—which could be seen in the heavens above at the time—and that if the group was to commit mass suicide its souls would be transferred to the alien craft, where all would be elevated to "a level of existence above human" (Wikipedia, 2009), turned out to be a shockingly easy task.

Between March 24th and 26th, Applewhite and his tragically-deluded clan—which ranged in ages from 26 to 72—committed suicide on the Heaven's Gate property at Rancho Santa Fe, California, via a deadly cocktail comprised of copious amounts of Phenobarbital and vodka, mixed with a liberal dash of applesauce; the latter was presumably added to give the concoction some much-needed taste. In addition, the group members also carefully positioned plastic bags over their heads, as a means to ensure asphyxiation, just in case the deadly drink failed to work. Applewhite, insanely overseeing the crazed affair, was the third-from-last to die.

For the most part, immersing oneself in the UFO arena is a relatively harmless—although very often life-changing—experience. As the affair of Heaven's Gate acutely demonstrates, however, sometimes the world of the flying saucer can be downright deadly. And, guess what: There was nary a report of the Space-Brothers shedding a single tear for the departed.

A farmer born in 1937 in the Swiss town of Bulach, Eduard "Billy" Meier has, without doubt, lived a most interesting life. While still in his teens he joined the French Foreign Legion, later traveled the world— covering more than 40 countries in 12 years as he pursued his deep interest in spiritual issues—and, in 1965, lost his left arm in a bus accident in Turkey. Meier also claims personal contacts with benevolent, human-like aliens that began way back in 1942, with an aged extraterrestrial named Sfath, and that continued until 1953, after which Sfath was replaced by a female alien named Asket, who remained in Meier's life until 1964. Then, for the next 11 years, there was nothing.

That all changed in January 1975, when Meier's place in the world of the Contactees was definitively established, after Sfath's granddaughter, Semjase, deemed him worthy of a visitation. As Meier tells the story, in that year he began receiving both telepathic messages and face-to-face contacts from a group of aliens that lived on a planet called Erra, which he maintains can be found in the star system that we call the Pleiades. Among Meier's chief contacts were Ptaah, Semjase, Quetzal, and Pleija. The people of Erra, says Meier, can live for up to 1,000 years, and the population of their planet is approximately 500,000,000—something that pales in comparison to the size of their overall "Federation" of 120 billion.

According to Meier's story, his alien friends charged him with certain consciousness-raising tasks. As he embarked upon his assigned mission, Meier says, he became the recipient of no less than 21 assassination attempts—some of which were supposedly initiated by hostile alien forces. This did not, however, stop him from establishing the Freie Interessengemeinschaft für Grenz- und Geisteswissenschaften und Ufologiestudien (the Free Community of Interests for the Fringe and Spiritual Sciences and UFOlogical Studies), a non-profit organization designed to further enlighten interested parties in the controversial world of the man himself.

Meier's claimed exchanges with the denizens of the Pleiades have reportedly been both intricate and varied, and have covered such issues as spirituality, the afterlife, the hazards posed by organized religious movements, the history of humankind, concerns of an environmental nature, ecology, and prophecies relative to the near future. There was a far more controversial claim too. According to Meier, along with an ex-Greek-Orthodox priest named Isa Rashid, he discovered south of the Old City of Jerusalem in 1963 a manuscript known as the *Talmud Jmmanuel*—described by its promoters as the source of the *Gospel of Matthew*, which is said to demonstrate extraterrestrial origins for *The Bible*.

Even more controversially, Meier maintains that on one occasion he traveled back in time—courtesy of his alien ally, Asket—to a point where he met personally with Jmmanuel, alleged to be the "real Jesus," and who informed the no doubt pleased Meier that Meier's level of evolution was greater than that of even Jmmanuel himself.

Meier's story also tells of two human males named Semjasa who influenced the Earth in much the same way as described in the *Book of Enoch*, a text that Meier maintains was altered for specifically religious purposes. The first Semjasa, says Meier, lived nearly 400,000 years ago and interbred with ancient humans, creating a specific lineage. The second Semjasa, Meier explains, lived around 9,000 BC, and was said to be the spirit-form of the original Semjasa, but one who inhabited the body of another human male: a survivor of the legendary land of Atlantis, who went on to seed yet another lineage—namely, one borne out of inter-breeding between the Atlanteans and the natives of North Africa, Mesopotamia, and Northern India.

As for the future that awaits us, Meier has stated on a number of occasions that we may be in for distinctly turbulent times. He went on record as saying that a Third World War would break out in either November 2006 or November 2008. It most definitely did not, of course. Now, he is saying 2010 and 2011 are the years when all hell may break loose across the globe—that is, unless we, as a species, change our warlike ways and elect to live in peace and harmony with one another. The future, says Meier, is not cast in stone.

16

Circles and Space-Brothers

In the late 1980s, there began a deep connection between the Space-Brothers and the largely British-based Crop Circle phenomenon. Precisely who, or what, is responsible for peppering the British landscape with the now-familiar Crop Circles, as well as the fantastically elaborate Pictograms—as they have come to be known—is a matter of deep conjecture, and one that has been hotly debated for years. Numerous theories have been advanced to try and explain the phenomenon; but opinions remain sharply divided. For some, Crop Circles are the work of benign extraterrestrials. Others see the spirit of the Earth itself—calling out to the people of the planet to change their destructive ways—as being wholly responsible. Then there is the notion that all of the Crop Circles have man-made origins. Whatever the ultimate truth of the matter, the phenomenon is one that shows no signs of disappearing anytime soon. But what of the link between the Space-Brothers and Crop Circles?

In a March 2009 article titled "Dog Walker Met UFO 'Alien' With Scandinavian Accent," journalist Sarah Knapton wrote in the pages of Britain's highly respected *Daily Telegraph* newspaper that the British Ministry of Defense had then-recently released into the public domain— via the terms of the nation's Freedom of Information Act—a number of formerly classified files on UFOs. One of those files, said Knapton, detailed the account in which "a dog walker claimed she met a man from another planet who said aliens were responsible for crop circles" (*Daily Telegraph*, 2009).

So the story went: The anonymous woman had telephoned the Royal Air Force base at Wattisham, Suffolk, in a state of considerable distress, and with a remarkable tale to tell. As the woman told the operator at the base, the incident in question had occurred while she was walking her dog on a sports field close to her home near the city of Norwich at about 10:30 p.m. on the night of November 20, 1989. She had been approached by a man with a "Scandinavian-type accent," who was dressed in "a light-brown garment like a flying suit" (Ibid.).

Royal Air Force documentation on the case notes: "He asked her if she was aware of stories about large circular flattened areas appearing in fields of wheat, and then went on to explain that he was from another planet similar to Earth, and that the circles had been caused by others like him who had traveled to Earth" (Ibid.).

The man assured the woman that the aliens were friendly, but that "they were told not to have contact with humans for fear that they would be considered a threat" (Ibid.).

Quite understandably, the woman said she was "completely terrified" by the encounter, and added that after about 10 minutes the strange man left. But things were not quite over: As the woman ran for the safety of her home, she heard a "loud buzzing noise" behind her and turned around to see "a large, glowing, orange-white, spherical object rising vertically" from behind a group of trees (Ibid.).

The Royal Air Force operator who took the statement from the woman said the conversation lasted about an hour and described it as a "genuine call" (Ibid.) But this was not to be the end of the connection between the Crop Circle mystery and apparent Space-Brother-based manifestations.

Every year, dozens of Crop Circles appear in the British Isles. Photo courtesy of Nick Redfern.

In the summer of 1990, when interest in Crop Circles in Britain reached fever-pitch levels, a woman named Vanessa Martin spent a week roaming around the English county of Wiltshire while trying valiantly to get to the bottom of the mystery. But rather than solve the riddle of the Crop Circles, her experiences arguably only add to the mystery and wonder.

For the first couple of days of her adventure, Martin made the historic village of Avebury, Wiltshire, her base of operations. While strolling around the ancient standing-stones of Avebury on the second morning of her trip, Martin says, "out of nowhere" a man approached her, and began to engage her in conversation about the Crop Circle riddle. Significantly, Martin adds that the man was "dressed in bright white overalls and had really long yellow hair" (Martin, 2008).

The man introduced himself as "either Heyoki or Hoyaki, one of the two; I forget which," explains Martin (Martin, 2008). Given the fact that she was specifically in Wiltshire to try to gain a deep understanding of the true nature of the Crop Circles, Martin was more than happy to chat with someone who seemed just as interested in the subject as she was. But the long-haired Heyoki or Hoyaki was not just interested: He claimed to have the answers to the riddle.

As Martin listened intently, the man told her that Crop Circles were, indeed, as many believe them to be, the work of benign extraterrestrials—from the planet Neptune, no less! Those same extraterrestrials, Martin recalls being told, "…were trying to make us think about the world and the environment by making patterns containing messages, but without landing in front of us. They were trying to help, he said. I asked him how he knew this, and he laughed really loud—almost mad. Then he told me I should think about this and let myself understand it and take it all in, and everything would be okay. And, I swear, right after that he just vanished. I looked away for only a second and he was gone, nowhere at all. There were a few other people in the stones [sic], and I asked if they had seen him or spoken to him, but no-one had" (Martin, 2008).

The mystery man would not stay missing for long, however. The following day, Martin says, she took a trip to one of Britain's most recognizable and historic monuments, Stonehenge.

Martin adds: "I was on one side of the road, where the fence is today, and he was on the other. He didn't speak to me, but just gave me a big smile, pointed at the sky, and actually curtsied—like in an old film, or something. So, he obviously recognized me from the day before. He had on the same outfit, and I laughed back and waved. It was strange: right at the time, and still now, I can't remember how he went away—if it was in a car or by walking. It was like at Avebury. He was there once and then he was gone" (Martin, 2008).

Martin's odd experience is one that falls very comfortably into the Contactee arena: There is the presence of an unusual-looking character, dressed in a one-piece outfit and sporting a head of long, blond hair. There is the visitor's absurd assertion that a planet in our own solar system—in this case, Neptune—is inhabited by advanced beings. There is the claim that the aliens are here with a specific, positive task in mmind. And, there is the near certainty (given the fact that the man seemed to have the ability to appear and vanish at will, and without anyone else in the vicinity having any apparent awareness of his presence) that Martin's experience occurred in some form of altered state of mind.

But, most significant of all was the name of Martin's confidante: Heyoki or Hoyaki—which is very similar to Heyoka. And who, or what, is Heyoka? He is a magical, trickster-style entity that is a part of the culture, folklore, and mythology of a Native American Indian tribe called the Lacota, the western most of the three Sioux groups that occupy land in North and South Dakota. To the Lacota people, Heyoka is a contrarian, a jester, who can use laughter to heal. It is also his role to play tricks and games, and by doing so he tries to provoke people into thinking about things in an unconventional fashion. His goal is to raise awareness and consciousness in those whose paths he crosses—which seems to be precisely what Heyoki/Hoyaki was attempting to achieve in Vanessa Martin.

Stonehenge: the site of a 1990 encounter with one of the Space-Brothers. Photo courtesy of Nick Redfern.

Interestingly, of George Adamski, Colin Bennett says: "He represents the magical trickster. He stands for the Fool in King Lear, the Jester in the Tarot pack, the homunculus in the alchemic vessel. Such things are all psychic elements within what Jung called participation mystique. In our doomed simple-minded materialism we have lost almost all trace of such magical transformations" (Bennett, 2009).

The links between Crop Circles and the Space-Brothers are still not over. On July 8, 2009, researcher Micah Hanks penned the following: "Bizarre reports involving strange new developments in crop circle activity stemming from Wiltshire, England are coming to the attention of media today, thanks to Colin Andrews, author of the new book *Government Circles*. I received an email from Colin earlier today, detailing an odd set of circumstances that occurred just yesterday near Silbury Hill, unique especially because of the apparent presence of 'strange humanoids' witnessed at the scene.

"The latest bizarre event took place yesterday morning, July 7th, at approximately 5 a.m.," said Hanks, who then quoted Andrews as saying. "A Wiltshire Police Sergeant was driving in his private car towards Marlborough on the A4 highway and about to pass Silbury Hill on his left. He looked to his right and witnessed three exceptionally tall beings inspecting the new crop circle which appeared there on the 5th July" (Hanks, 2009).

The officer stopped his vehicle at this point, watching the "Nordic" beings for several minutes—chiefly because "they stood out as odd." According to the report, "Each of them were more than 6 feet tall, each had blond hair and also they all were wearing one piece white suites, with hoods that had been dropped onto the back of their heads" (Hanks, 2009).

After the officer shouted in the direction of the three men, and failed to receive any sort of acknowledgment, he ventured into the field in pursuit, at which time the three most assuredly did take notice of him: they proceeded to run away at a fantastic speed.

"I recognized that I could never catch up with them… they ran so exceptionally fast," the officer is reported to have told investigators, and while claiming to have felt "very uneasy" as he left the scene (Hanks, 2009).

Hanks expanded: "According to statistics presented by Peter Monaghan in 1994, Europeans and Latin Americans are several times more likely to report encountering a Nordic alien than a Grey,' the popular aliens in abductee lore here in the U.S. In fact, the European nation with the highest proportion of reported encounters with Nordic aliens is the United Kingdom, where so many of these recent crop circles have appeared" (Ibid.).

17

Altered States

One of the most significant aspects of countless Contactee-driven accounts is the fact that the experiences at issue occurred in significantly altered states of mind, and while the Contactees were often situated in distinctly isolated locations. Let us examine the evidence. As noted in Chapter 1, an early Contactee encounter that was brought to the attention of the FBI occurred in August 1947, and involved a Mr. Jones of Los Angeles. According to Jones's story, around 10 a.m. on the day at issue he had hiked into the mountains and was laying on the ground when he observed about one-half block away from him a large, silver, metal object that was greenish in color. Thereafter, Jones's mind became dominated by thoughts relative to extraterrestrial concerns about our burgeoning atomic technology. This was a trend that was only set to continue.

Samuel Eaton Thompson's tale of the March 28, 1950 encounter with multiple aliens in the woods of Washington State occurred after he fell tired, and was forced to rest for a while. And Truman Bethurum's encounters with curvy Captain Aura Rhanes began after Bethurum decided to "take a little snooze" while parked on Mormon Mesa in the early hours of a 1952 morning (Bethurum, 1970).

Skeptically minded souls might offer the opinion that Jones, Eaton and Bethurum merely fell asleep and experienced particularly vivid dreams of a UFO-like nature. Such a scenario is not impossible: Hypnagogia is a term that was coined in the 1800s by a French scholar named Alfred Maury. However, it has a history that extends long before Maury came on the scene: References to this strange condition can be found in the writings of the Greek philosopher Aristotle; in the works of the English Elizabethan occultist, astrologer, and herbalist Simon Forman; and in the written output of the Italian renaissance mathematician and physician Gerolamo Cardano. So, with that said, precisely what is hypnagogia?

Basically, it's a term that describes the stage between wakefulness and sleep—a stage in the sleep process that may be dominated by a wide and infinitely varied body of sensory experiences. For example, those in hypnagogic states have reported hearing voices ranging from barely audible whispers to wild screams. Others have heard random snatches of speech— largely nonsensical, but occasionally containing unusual fictional names (not unlike some of those used by the Space-Brothers, it could be argued), and others have seen disembodied heads, or what appear to be fully formed entities in their bedrooms. Humming, roaring, hissing, rushing, and buzzing noises are also frequently reported by people experiencing hypnagogia.

It is not out of the question that some claims of Contactee-type encounters could have been due to hypnagogia—remember that Truman Bethurum's initial experience atop Mormon Mesa was initiated after he was groggily awoken by "what I can only describe as mumbling," which is a classic facet of hypnagogia (Bethurum, 1954). But, as is the case with so many aspects of the Contactee enigma, the matter is not so clear cut. It appears to be the case that the phenomenon that is responsible for encounters of the Contactee kind has the ability to induce radically altered states of mind, perception, and awareness, including hypnagogia. It may do so to ensure that the witness perceives the phenomena in a fashion that accords with a pre-planned agenda based around communication, manipulation of the mind, and control of the audio-visual senses. In other words, even if hypnagogia does play a role in the Contactee arena, it may be an induced role, rather than one that always occurs purely at random—as will become clear later.

Let us now focus our attention on George Van Tassel of Giant Rock and Integratron infamy. As longtime Contactee Robert Short noted, when he visited Giant Rock in 1953, initial contact with Van Tassel's allegedly alien entities was achieved not via scanning the stars with powerful telescopes. Rather, matters commenced via distinctly different means: "We're chanting to raise the vibrations," Mrs. Van Tassel told Short, as the night's proceedings began (Short, 2003).

Certainly, Van Tassel was very open about the fact that meditation was a vital component of his interactions with the Space-Brothers. Meditation, in essence, is a mental discipline by which one attempts to get beyond the reflexive, thinking mind into a deep state of relaxation or awareness, and is a component of numerous religions, including Buddhism, Islam, Christianity, Judaism, and Hinduism. When the chanting was over, noted Short: "…George Van Tassel began to speak. But then something even stranger happened. Momentarily, his voice changed…became deeper, a monotone. Whoever was speaking through him now introduced himself as some space being!" (Short, 2003).

The process is known as channeling—an altered state in which the participant enters a trance, or leaves his or her body and subsequently becomes "possessed" by a specific entity, such as a long-haired alien, a demon, the spirit of a deceased loved one—you take your pick—who then speaks through him or her, often in a radically altered voice, while offering words of wisdom, spiritual comfort, or utter deceit. A practically-identical scenario has been noted by researcher Sean Devney, in relation to the contacts of George Hunt Williamson. Quoting eyewitnesses to Williamson's actions, Devney says: "When Williamson started to channel, it was something truly inexplicable. [He] would begin speaking in several different voices, one right after the other" (Hiddell, 1995).

Moving on from hypnagogia, meditation, and channeling, there is another issue that may offer some answers concerning claims of alien contact. It revolves around the ingestion of mind-altering substances. Dimethyltryptamine—or DMT—is a naturally occurring tryptamine and potent psychedelic drug that can be found not just in numerous plants, but also, in trace amounts at least, within the human body, where its natural function is presently undetermined. Smoking or injecting DMT has been shown to produce vivid and extraordinary hallucinations—some of which have a major bearing on the issue of extraterrestrial encounters.

Researcher Micah Hanks says:

The notion that something from within our bodies could be considered an illegal substance seems rather odd to me. However, this is very much the case with DMT, an active ingredient in the mysterious shamanic ayahuasca tea used by native cultures around the world for vision quests.

The catch is that we don't know exactly where the DMT is created, though pioneering psychedelics researcher Dr. Rick Strassman has suggested that, in theory, the stuff could be produced within the human pineal gland, which Renee Descartes famously proposed 'was the point of mediation between the material body and the immaterial soul.'"

Continuing, Hanks notes:

Recent studies by University of Wisconsin-Madison researchers found that DMT regulates a mysterious protein that is abundant throughout the body called the sigma-1 receptor. Experiments with laboratory mice that had had this receptor genetically removed yielded the strange effect of nothing; whereas 'normal' mice that had been injected with DMT yielded expected increases in hyperactivity until the effects of the drug had worn off. Indeed, it seems that a receptor for the hallucinogenic effects of DMT may have been discovered.

Many of the shamanic cultures around the world who use DMT-rich snuffs and teas in their rituals describe entities they meet while taking the stuff. Similarly, test subjects in various DMT studies, including those of Rick Strassman, report meeting similar 'beings.' And common to both groups are haunting consistencies between descriptions of these entities. In fact, some believe these beings could even be 'inter-dimensional ambassadors' which come to meet psychonauts in the sub-space realm that lingers between reality and wherever people experiencing a DMT trip tend to end up visiting.

Hanks concludes: "We are left with the curious, even frightening, questions as to how exactly drugs like DMT work, why it exists in the human body, and how, under the right conditions, substances like this might bear strange abilities that allow us some limited perception of those things which exist in places from beyond" (Hanks, 2009).

Greg Bishop has also commented on the research and studies into the effects of DMT as undertaken by the aforementioned Dr. Rick Strassman: "From 1990 to 1995, Strassman worked with 60 volunteers at the University of New Mexico. Assisted by hospital nurses, he administered DMT intravenously to the subjects, and sat by to observe and record the reactions. There was also extensive debriefing after the sessions to note anything that was not described vocally during the drug trips. About half of the volunteers met up with something that they described as 'alien' during their experiences" (Bishop, 2007).

In June 2008, Bishop met with Strassman and asked the doctor if it was possible that some of his test-subjects might have had prior knowledge of the alien-encounter motif, and which might have adversely colored their experiences. Bishop notes that in response to his question "…Strassman assured me that not only had some not known the details of reported UFO abductions, but that he knew of accounts from cultures who have had little or no contact with civilization that also described UFOs and alien-like entities while under the influence of psychoactive plants, and that this had occurred before contact with those from outside of their culture" (Bishop, 2008).

Bishop adds that the doctor wrote: "When reviewing my bedside notes, I continually feel surprise in seeing how many of our volunteers 'made contact' with 'them,' or other beings…Research subjects used expressions like 'entities,' 'beings,' 'aliens,' 'guides,' and 'helpers' to describe them. The 'life forms' looked like clowns, reptiles, mantises, bees, spiders, cacti, and stick figures" (Ibid.).

Greg Bishop rightly says with respect to the above: "…these phrases and descriptions are exactly what is [sic] reported by people who claim to have been taken out of their beds or cars or wherever and led onto machines that looked like spaceships" (Ibid.).

He adds: "The fundamentalist skeptic stirs, rises, and grumbles, 'See? It is all in the mind.' Those with any semblance of an inquiring and reasonably independent disposition cannot deny the parallels. I cannot claim any abduction experiences, either straight or on drugs; but the data intersections are intriguing, and point to a need for a revised view of just what this alien encounter thing is all about" (Ibid.).

Bishop advises those with an interest in such matters to "call up the aliens if you want. All you need is a good connection" (Ibid.).

Then there is the altered-state experience of Fortean investigator and author Adam Gorightly, who, in December 1986, penned the following letter to British UFO researcher Jenny Randles.

Dear Ms. Jenny Randles,

I would like to relate an experience that happened to myself and a colleague in 1979 in Fresno, Calif. Let me preface this statement by saying that we were under the influence of the hallucinogenic drug, LSD. But hear me out: these are not the ravings of a drug-saturated fruitcake; I am not a habitual drug user, nor have I used LSD for several years. But to deny that I was not under its influence when this incident occurred would be to give an incomplete account of what transpired on that fateful night.

On the night in question—fully under the influence of said drug—we observed several 'flying saucers,' in several shapes, sizes, and multicolored variations. I am not denying that what we saw were hallucinations, but if they were, then they were 'dual hallucinations,' for we both saw the same sights and sounds.

Now, a brief description of this event: The sighting occurred along a levee located in a residential section of town. Before we arrived at the levee (we were on foot) we joked to ourselves about how we might see a UFO during our little 'trip.' We laughed to ourselves (somewhat uncontrollably) how no one would ever believe us due to the condition we were in.

Anyway, after walking a short time on the levee, we saw our first 'UFO.' The sight of this made me fall to one knee and we were both astounded by its sight. During the course of the night we saw several, anywhere from six to eight. One was cigar shaped, some saucer shaped, one with a multi-colored propeller. This all occurred in the span of not more than an hour and a half, I think, though the passing of time was hard to estimate due to the effects of the drug. The last one we saw appeared like a falling star in the sky that seemed to stop in mid-descent, then turned into a space ship, or whatever it was. After the sighting of this 'UFO' we turned around and headed back, the way we came.

Now I realize the descriptions I am giving are sketchy, but in retrospect it seemed almost like a dream, everything happening so fast. If I were to describe every little detail, I'd be here all night. So I'll try to wrap it up and sum up the experience in a few more words.

When we arrived back at the point where we saw the first UFO, a beam of light shot down directly in front of us some 50 yards away, emanating from nothing we could see. I said, 'Wow, did you see that?' and my colleague responded that he saw it, too. Of course, we said things like, 'Wow, did you see that?' and, 'Oh, my God!' many times that night. Through the whole experience, we felt a presence communicating non-verbally to us. Obviously, we were the only ones who saw 'them.' There were many houses in the vicinity, with many people living there who could have seen 'them,' but it appears that 'they' were for our eyes only. Perhaps 'they' were hallucinations, but if they were, it was a 'dual hallucination,' for we both saw the same thing (Gorightly, 1986).

Gorightly's communication to Randles is significant on several points. Number one: Entering into an undoubted altered state of mind via the use of hallucinogenic substances allowed Gorightly and his friend to experience the UFO phenomenon at close quarters, and in a fashion that was seemingly inaccessible to—or at least unseen by—anyone else in the vicinity whose mind was not radically transformed.

Second, Gorightly's comment that "…through the whole experience, we felt a presence communicating non-verbally to us…" (Gorightly, 1986) cannot be ignored. It surely places the pair's experience in the arena of contact with an undeniable unknown. Gorightly has never forgotten this 30-year-old life-changing experience.

Today, he says of the Contactee issue: "When you look at some of the stories of people like Menger, Bethurum, Adamski, and so on, there's not much proof there; but I sense at the core of their experiences that something profound happened to some of those guys to push them forward and create that whole movement. I suspect it's not necessarily E.T.'s; but something that has been with us forever: the Native American trickster, fairy-lore; maybe it's an energy that can be good or bad. There's definitely evidence of the phenomenon changing people—individually and as a group. Adamski, for instance, whether it was all made up or not, had a profound impact on thousands of people. But I doubt that it's just as simple as nuts-and-bolts spaceships and aliens. It's more of a religious, mystical thing" (Gorightly, 2009).

Covering similar territory to that described to Jenny Randles by Adam Gorightly is the testimony of the late author and visionary Terence McKenna. While undertaking research into—and actively participating in—the effects of psychedelics on the human body and mind in the Amazon Jungle in the 1960s, McKennna was advised by one of his contacts to sit down, and "watch a portion of the sky where, reportedly, a UFO might appear" (Dr. Fong's House of Mysteries, 2009). After a while, and as the psychedelics took effect, Mckenna, to his astonishment, saw a "strange, thin, horizontal cloud forming near the horizon" (Ibid.). The cloud grew in length; it then divided in two, before finally recombining and appearing directly overhead. But, as the phenomenon got ever closer, Mckenna could see it was no cloud. Rather, it was nothing less than a flying saucer of the exact type that Orthon would have been proud to pilot.

McKenna stated later: "I recognized this thing. It looked like the end cap of a Hoover vacuum cleaner; exactly the same fake saucer as in George Adamski's photos. This thing flew right over my head, and it was as phony as a three-dollar bill. I knew it was a fake" (Ibid.).

McKenna could only suggest that non-human entities from a realm that was either psychic or alien in origin were having fun with him—while he was high on psychedelics—by appearing in the one form that was most likely to confound his intellectual sensibilities.

Finally, we come to a case that has definite Space-Brother-based overtones to it: It includes reference to what may have been a classic hypnagogic experience; it has uncanny parallels with the story of Truman Bethurum; and it involves the sighting of a human-like, angelic-looking figure that could just as easily have stepped out of one of the saucers that landed before

An 1893 engraving of Joseph Smith and the angel Moroni.

Adamski, Van Tassel, Short, and countless other Contactees in the 1950s. Except for one thing: This is a story that had its origins in the early 1800s, and led to the formation of one of the world's major religions.

Joseph Smith, Jr., born on December 23, 1805, was the founder of the Latter Day Saint movement, more commonly known as Mormonism. In 1827, Smith began to develop a not-insubstantial following after he proclaimed that an angel named Moroni had visited him (as it significantly transpires, late one night, while he slept) and directed him to a book—inscribed on a set of golden plates—that supposedly detailed a visit of Jesus Christ to the Americas.

The book, Moroni said, was buried on a hill near Smith's home, which was variously referred to as Cumorah Hill and Mormon Hill. Three years later, Smith published—under the title of the *Book of Mormon*—what he said was a translation of these plates. The Church of Jesus Christ of Latter Day Saints was duly born.

How curious that more than 120 years after Smith's experience, Truman Bethurum underwent a series of astonishingly similar encounters. His 1952 liaisons with other-worldly entities occurred atop the similarly named Mormon Mesa. Just like Smith, Bethurum's first encounter began when his sleep was disturbed by the sudden presence of a superior being—or beings, in Bethurum's case. In a similar fashion to the way in which Moroni told Smith that the priceless manuscript that ultimately became the *Book of Mormon* was "inscribed" on a set of golden plates, so on one occasion Bethurum was also the recipient of (to him, at least) a priceless inscription: the so-called Clarionites "dropped a small flare" near an old power line that skirted the hills northeast of Glendale that was intended for Bethurum's attention. On retrieving the flare, Bethurum said that close by was a foot-square package that had a four-word note inscribed on its outside: "To Truman From Aura" (Bethurum, 1970).

Finally, an 1893 engraving by Edward Stevenson showing the angel Moroni delivering the plates to Smith atop Mormon Hill displays Moroni bathed in a brightly glowing aura. Taking into consideration the clear similarities between the experiences of Smith and those of Bethurum—both of which had an air of altered-states and the unreal about them—and with Edward Stevenson's brightly shining image fixed firmly in our minds, one might be inclined to say that Bethurum's shapely Captain Aura Rhanes truly had an aura that reigned.

But there is a problem: Despite the undeniable parallels between each story, Smith was told that his visitor was an angelic being named Moroni, whereas Aura Rhanes confidently assured the trusting Bethurum that she was an astronaut from the (non-existent) planet Clarion. Someone was being highly economical with the truth—or: both men were being carefully manipulated while in susceptible, altered states. But by whom and for what purpose?

Terence McKenna said of experiencing contact with entities of alien, discarnate, or equally exotic, yet not-fully-understood, origins: "It is no great accomplishment to hear a voice in the head. The accomplishment is to make sure that it is telling you the truth" (Bishop, 2007). That is the critical issue at stake in the cases of Bethurum and Smith, and which also faces us in the following chapters: determining the nature of what lies at the heart of the Contactee puzzle, ascertaining how it utilizes altered states to achieves its aims, and understanding to what extent it is being truthful with us—or not—about its origins, its motivations, its appearance, and much more.

As astonishing as it may seem, there appear to be two distinct phenomena at work when it comes to the world of the Contactee: one that is orchestrated and controlled by elements of the intelligence communities, military bodies, and defense agencies of several nations, and one that is, in literal terms, truly alien. More astonishing, both phenomena seem to make use of altered states of mind to achieve their unusual goals of life-changing proportions.

18

Space Aliens or Secret Agents?

One of the strangest, and certainly most controversial, theories postulated to explain the tales of Adamski, Van Tassel, and their ilk suggests they were the unwitting players in a top secret Kremlin plot designed to make the United States believe that outer space was populated by civilizations of a distinctly communist nature. Notably, dark tales of communist links to the early Contactees did indeed proliferate. This possibility was definitely of concern to a Yucca Valley resident who, on August 5, 1954, wrote to the FBI suggesting that George Van Tassel be investigated to determine if he was working as a Soviet spy.

Similarly, in its files on George Adamski, the FBI noted in 1953 that:

Adamski made the prediction that Russia will dominate the world and we will then have an era of peace for 1,000 years. He stated that Russia already has the atom bomb and the hydrogen bomb and that the great earthquake, which was reported behind the Iron Curtain recently, was actually a hydrogen bomb explosion being tried out by the Russians. Adamski states this 'earthquake' broke seismograph machines and he added that no normal earthquake can do that.

Adamski stated that within the next 12 months, San Diego will be bombed. Adamski stated that it does not make any difference if the United States has more atom bombs than Russia inasmuch as Russia needs only 10 atom bombs to cripple the United States by placing these simultaneously on such spots as Chicago and other vital centers of this country. The United States today is in the same state of deterioration as was the Roman Empire prior to its collapse and it will fall just as the Roman Empire did. The Government in this country is a corrupt form of government and capitalists are enslaving the poor (FBI, 1953).

Only a year or so after his claimed encounters with Space Captain Aura Rhanes of the planet Clarion, Truman Bethurum stated the following: "Two or three fellows who had sons in Korea and who read a lot in the newspapers about the Communist underground in this country, were convinced in their own minds that I was, if making contact with anyone at all, making it with enemy agents. They even went so far as to tell me belligerently that they intended to get guns and follow me nights, and if they caught up me having intercourse with any people from planes, airships of any kind, they'd blast me and those people too" (Bethurum, 1954). On a related matter, FBI records demonstrate that in December 1954, the Palm Springs Republican Club contacted the FBI to inquire if Bethurum might be guilty of "trying to put over any propaganda" (FBI, 1954).

Then there are the recollections of Jim Moseley. In his own words, in the early-to-mid 1950s, "...I had fallen under the influence of Charles Samwick, a retired army intelligence officer...Quite sincere and most convincing, he told me...'the Communist Party has planted an agent in every civilian saucer club in the United States'" (Moseley, 2002). Similarly, in his *Saucer News* publication of June-July 1955, Moseley commented thus:

"...Let us give some very serious consideration to the many alleged space men being called to the public's attention—all of whom invariably

Jim Moseley, a long-time researcher and observer of the Contactee scene. Photo courtesy of Nick Redfern.

tell us of the dangers of war and the exploitation of atomic energy. No one desires peace any more sincerely than we do, but let us remember too that it is part of the Communist 'peace line' to frighten the American people into ceasing our atomic experiments. It is quite possible that some of these 'space men' are unwittingly playing into the hands of the Communists" (Moseley, 1955).

Moseley makes a very important point with respect to the Contactee movement in the United States, and which may help to explain why a significant degree of concern was shown at an official level about the politics of the players on the scene: "Adamski and the Contactees represented an early hippy philosophy of the time—a 1950s version of what came later in the Sixties with flower-power [and] protests. A lot of what they were saying merged into the mainstream of liberal thinking at that time. So, in that way, it was a very significant movement" (Moseley, 2009).

Evidence that an element of the British Police Force called Special Branch took an interest in the Contactees because of communist-related concerns is now in the public domain, thanks to the persistent research of UFO investigators Andy Roberts and David Clarke, who have uncovered once-secret Special Branch files on our old friend George King of the

Aetherius Society. As the files demonstrate, in the latter part of the 1950s, King became a well-known character to Special Branch, but for reasons that had little to do with flying saucers—directly, at least.

Roberts and Clarke learned from now-declassified Special Branch documentation that in both August 1958 and August 1959, Special Branch operatives secretly attended Aetherius Society demonstrations in London. Special Branch recorded that: "…it can thus be seen that the Aetherius society is molding its preposterous claims to conform with the popular concepts of religion…There is a possibility that all this high-sounding talk of 'Karma' and 'Cosmic Parliaments' is simply a system of financial gain for certain individuals and George King in particular" (Clarke, 2007).

Moreover, Roberts and Clarke cite one particularly important Special Branch document from the same era that states the Aetherius Society was "still active in its campaign against nuclear weapon tests, and in this respect its policy is closely allied with that of the Communist Party" (Ibid.). As all of this demonstrates, Special Branch was most certainly taking notice of King and Co., but not for reasons that had any direct bearing on the Contactee controversy. Rather, it was for other, more down-to-earth reasons and concerns relative to politics and groups perceived as being troublesome and/or subversive by the establishment of the day—such as the Communist Party.

A variation on the communist angle is one that suggests the Contactees were in the clandestine employ of the United States' Intelligence community. Their secret role: to spread outlandish—and utterly fictitious—tales of trips to the moon and Venus with long-haired aliens. Their purpose: to make the entire UFO subject seem ridiculous, and to bury the truly unexplained and mystifying reports amongst a mass of largely unbelievable tales of cosmic contact. As controversial as it may seem, when we look for connections between the Contactees and elements of U.S. officialdom, we do find them.

As has been demonstrated, the FBI of the 1950s was hardly enamored of George Van Tassel, but that was not always the case. The Freedom of Information Act has shown that in previous years Van Tassel had what could be termed quasi-official links with the FBI that were most assuredly not frowned upon. An FBI document of November 16, 1954, for example, references Van Tassel as having been "acquainted" with FBI Special Agent Walter Bott (who had then recently died), and that furthermore Van Tassel "helped [Bott] on many cases at Lockheed" (FBI, 1954).

In addition to that startling revelation, as has been noted earlier, while employed with Hughes Aircraft, Van Tassel acted in an assistance capacity to none other than Howard Hughes himself. In 1977, an astonishing book, *The Hughes Papers* by Elaine Davenport, Paul Eddy, and Mark Huwitz, was published and disclosed a wealth of hitherto unknown material pertaining to Hughes, including his deep connections to the CIA. This does not, of course, link Van Tassel with the CIA in any capacity, but it is food for thought nevertheless.

Moving on to George Adamski, researcher George Andrews says: "People who traveled with Adamski noticed that he had been issued a special passport, such as is usually reserved for diplomats and high government officials. It is entirely possible that he may have been a CIA disinformation agent who successfully fulfilled the mission of making the subject of UFOs seem so absurd that no independent in-depth investigation would be made by qualified academics" (Andrews, 1986).

And there is more to come. In 1954, a group of West Coast–based Contactees—including both Truman Bethurum and George Hunt Williamson—gave a series of lectures at the Hotel Gibson in Cincinnati. As this was also the home city of the UFO researcher Leonard Stringfield, paths inevitably crossed. Hoping to get Stringfield to endorse their talks, Bethurum, Williamson, and their flock called at his home and introduced themselves. Stringfield flatly refused to lend his support, although he did invite the group into his home. It was while in the company of the Contactees that Stringfield had an intriguing experience, as he noted later:

"After their departure I began to wonder about their causes. At one point during the evening's many tête-à-têtes, I chanced to overhear two members discussing the FBI. Pretending aloofness, I tried to overhear more. It seemed that one person was puzzling over the presence of an 'agent' in the group. When I was caught standing too close, the FBI talk stopped. Whether or not I had reason to be suspicious, it was not difficult for me to believe that some of the Contactees behind all this costly showmanship were official 'plants'" (Stringfield, 1978).

Finally, there is the tale of Howard Menger, author of the book *From Outer Space to You*. As the late and renowned Fortean authority John Keel noted in letters to the UFO researcher Gray Barker and *Saucer Smear* editor Jim Moseley, Menger termed his book "fiction-fact" and implied that the Pentagon had asked him to participate in an experiment to test the public's reaction to extra terrestrial contact (Keel, 1971).

19

Manipulating the Mind

Although many UFO researchers who have immersed themselves within the world of the Contactees have been content to conclude that the claims at issue are either basically true or manifestly bogus, there is yet another avenue that may have a key bearing on resolving certain aspects of the subject, yet it is one that is seldom addressed—namely, that of U.S. military-sponsored "mind control."

Within the annals of research into conspiracy theories, there is perhaps no more emotive term than that of mind control. Mentioning those two words to anyone who has even a remote awareness of their meaning will invariably provoke graphic imagery and commentary pertaining to political assassinations, dark and disturbing CIA chicanery, and hypnotically controlled killers. Indeed, the specter of mind control is one that has firmly worked its ominous way into numerous facets of modern-day society.

Although the U.S. intelligence community, military and government have undertaken countless official (and off-the-record, too) projects pertaining to mind control, without any doubt whatsoever the most notorious of all was Project MK-Ultra: a clandestine operation that operated out of the CIA's Office of Scientific Intelligence, and that had its beginnings in the Cold War era of the late 1940s and very early 1950s.

To demonstrate the level of secrecy that surrounded Project MK-Ultra, even though it had kicked off years before, its existence was largely unknown outside of the intelligence world until 1975—when the Church Committee and the Rockefeller Commission began making their own investigations of the CIA's mind control related activities. The story that unfolded was both dark and disturbing. The scope of the project was spelled out in an August 1977 document titled *The Senate MK-Ultra Hearings* that was prepared by the Senate Select Committee on Intelligence and the Committee on Human Resources, as a result of its probing into the secret and dark world of the CIA.

The author of the document explained: "Research and development programs to find materials which could be used to alter human behavior were initiated in the late 1940s and early 1950s. These experimental programs originally included testing of drugs involving witting human subjects, and culminated in tests using unwitting, non-volunteer human subjects. These tests were designed to determine the potential effects of chemical or biological agents when used operationally against individuals unaware that they had received a drug" (Senate Select Committee, 1977).

The Committee was highly disturbed to learn that with respect to the mind control and mind-manipulation projects, the CIA's normal administrative controls were controversially waived for programs involving chemical and biological agents—supposedly to protect their security, but more likely to protect those CIA personnel who knew they were verging upon breaking the law.

It is, perhaps, the following statement from the Committee that demonstrates the level of controversy that surrounded, and that still surrounds, the issue of mind control based projects: "The decision to institute one of the Army's LSD field testing projects had been based, at least in part, on the finding that no long-term residual effects had ever resulted from the drug's administration. The CIA's failure to inform the

Army of a death which resulted from the surreptitious administration of LSD to unwitting Americans, may well have resulted in the institution of an unnecessary and potentially lethal program" (Senate Select Committee, 1977).

What does any of this have to do with the controversial tales of the Contactees? To answer that question we have to turn our attention back to the strange story of Orfeo Angelucci. First, however, a little vital and relevant background is required on a man named Frank Olson: a chemist with the U.S. Army's Special Operations Division at Fort Detrick, Maryland, who—at the time of his still-controversial death on the night of November 28, 1953—was working on issues pertaining to sophisticated mind-controlling drugs and biological weaponry.

According to the government's official version of events, some time before his death, and as part of the MK-Ultra experimentation, Olson had, without his knowledge and consent, been dosed with LSD and subsequently suffered from both extreme paranoia and a mental collapse. As a result, the CIA quickly put him under the care of a New York–based psychiatrist who worked with the Agency, and who strongly recommended that Olson be placed into a mental institution for recovery. On his last night in Manhattan, however, tragedy struck: Olson reportedly threw himself out of a 10th-floor hotel room window, not surprisingly dying upon impact.

Scandalously, Olson's family had no knowledge of the details of the accident until the Rockefeller Commission began its inquiries into the strange world of MK-Ultra. As a result, in 1975, the government grudgingly admitted that Olson had indeed been hit with LSD without his knowledge and duly offered his family an out-of-court settlement of $750,000—which they accepted. But the story was not over.

In 1994, Olson's son, Eric, had his father's body exhumed. The forensic scientist in charge of the examination, George Washington University Professor James E. Starrs, determined that Olson had suffered from some form of blunt-force trauma to his forehead prior to falling out of the broken window, but exhibited no visible laceration indicating that he had fallen through a broken window. Not surprisingly, the evidence was termed "rankly and starkly suggestive of homicide" (Wikipedia, 2009). Based on the findings of Professor Starrs, in 1996, the Manhattan District Attorney opened a homicide investigation into Olson's death, but was unable to find enough evidence to bring charges.

And, that all brings us to back Orfeo Angelucci.

Although Angelucci's claims of alien contact have been viewed as the literal truth or merely the stuff of overwhelming fantasy, with the benefit of hindsight, there are reasons for thinking that at least some of the man's experiences may have been the result of clandestine, LSD-based MK-Ultra-style activity. In other words, integral parts of Angelucci's story may have had less to do with literal extraterrestrials, and far more to do with hallucinogenic drugs and secret government operations.

It should not go amiss that Angelucci's strange and surreal experiences with the decidedly mysterious Adam occurred only after Angelucci was required to ingest a liquid of unknown origin and nature—but one that had distinctly profound effects upon his mental state. With this in mind, consider the following, relevant quotes from Angelucci that highlight his famous encounter with Adam at Tiny's Diner, and that I have held back from relating in full until now, chiefly because of the direct relevance that his words have to the subject-matter of this chapter.

…I took the pellet and dropped it into my glass. Immediately the water bubbled, turning slowly into the clear, pale amber contained in [Adam's] own glass. I lifted the glass a few inches from the table, looking into it with a feeling that this might be the drink I dared not hope for. The exhilarating aroma rising from it could not be mistaken.

…I thrilled from head to foot as I took the glass, lifted it to my lips, and swallowed twice from it. At that instant, I entered, with Adam, into a more exalted state and everything around me took on a different semblance. No longer was I in Tiny's café in Twentynine Palms. It had been transformed into a cozy retreat on some radiant star system. Though everything remained in its same position, added beauty and meaning were given to the things and people present there.

…Among the patrons dining that evening were two marines from the nearby base. Sometimes they glanced our way as they talked and drank beer following their meal.

The first two sips had done all that a river of the nectar could do…As we lingered over our dessert, Adam persisted in staring at the glass which seemed to have filled itself with the strange liquid. I could feel that his almost mesmerized interest in the glass was fraught with expectancy. Were my ears deceiving me? Was that music I heard coming from the direction of the glass? It must be music. No sound could be so enchanting unless played by some skilled musician.

…Then slowly I too looked at the glass and was held in amazement. A miniature young woman was dancing in the nectar! Her golden-blond beauty was as arresting as the miracle of her projection in the glass. Her arms moved in rhythmic motion with the graceful thrusts of her dancing body. Her feet were so light and responsive that the music itself seemed to emanate from them… Soon the liquid in the glass lowered to the halfway point. It was being drained away as mysteriously as it had been brought in. The two young marines were looking toward our table very intently (Angelucci, 1955 and 1959).

Although some may disagree, Angelucci's tale bears all the hallmarks of someone taking a long and winding trip of the definitively chemical kind: After taking a drink, says Angelucci, the previously innocuous restaurant is "transformed into a cozy retreat on some radiant star system" (Ibid.). Needless to say, this is not the experience that most people report upon taking a gulp or several of a drink in the average American diner.

"Added beauty and meaning" are suddenly given to all things around Angelucci, as his radically-transformed mind begins to excitedly navigate previously uncharted realms. He hears captivating music that prompts him to comment: "No sound could be so enchanting unless played by some skilled musician" (Ibid.).

Most graphic of all, and surely indicative of a strange journey down Hallucinogenic Lane, is Angelucci's assertion that he witnessed a "miniature young woman…dancing in the nectar! Her golden-blond beauty was as arresting as the miracle of her projection in the glass. Her arms moved in rhythmic motion with the graceful thrusts of her dancing body" (Ibid.).

And what are we to make of "the two young marines [who] were looking toward our table very intently"? (Ibid.). Was the pair, perhaps, present to monitor the situation, and to ensure that things did not get out of hand—as had happened so tragically with Frank Olson only a couple of years earlier? If it is the case that Angelucci's experiences with Adam were indeed sponsored by some agency of the official world—such as the CIA, which was deeply implicated in the Olson affair—then a key question needs to be asked: What was the motivation behind such bizarre activity?

To provide a possible answer to that conundrum, we need to return to the world of communism. In his early writings, Angelucci briefly talked about a mysterious "subversive element" who he met with while "on my tour of the East," and who tried "to convert me to Communism and slant my talks along the Party Line" (Angelucci, 1955). In view of this revelation, it might be wise to consider the very real possibility that Angelucci's experiences with Adam had absolutely nothing whatsoever to do with what may have been earlier, genuinely anomalous encounters.

If elements of the U.S. government, military, and intelligence community were concerned that some of the very early Contactees were acting as mouthpieces for communism, it makes sense that those same elements might have wished to ascertain the motivations of each and every one of the early Contactees at an up-close-and-personal level. Taking into consideration the fact that Angelucci openly admitted to having been approached by a "subversive element" that attempted to, in his own words, "convert me to Communism and slant my talks along the Party Line," such a possibility makes even more sense.

And, what better way for the men in black suits to cover their tracks than to seduce Angelucci into a drug-fuelled state of wonder, enlightenment and openness, all the time carefully noting, logging, and assessing his character and motivations—and with a couple of military personnel sat nearby, just in case the LSD-fuelled experience went catastrophically awry? A sobering thought, to say the very least; and one that may have profound implications for the whole Contactee controversy. It's made all the more controversial by virtue of the fact that it is not an isolated case: It's time for us to once again acquaint ourselves with Antonio Villas Boas. But just before doing so, we should muse carefully on the words of one of the world's leading authorities on UFOs, Dr. Jacques Vallee, who has written extensively about the way in which the phenomenon may have been manipulated by wholly terrestrial forces:

While the hypothesis of alien contact is an exciting one, justified on the basis of continuing observations of unidentified flying objects, it carries the potential for exploitation and manipulation by deceptive groups with their own hidden agenda.

I believe that UFOs are physically real. They represent a fantastic technology controlled by an unknown form of consciousness. But I also believe that it would be dangerous to jump to premature conclusions about their origin and nature, because the phenomenon serves as the vehicle for images that can be manipulated to promote belief systems tending to the long-term transformation of human society (Vallee, 2008).

Keep Vallee's words firmly in mind as you read on.

20

Inventing Aliens

Rich Reynolds is a longtime investigative-researcher of and astute commentator on the UFO scene as well as its many attendant players, mysteries, and controversies. He's also someone with a remarkable account to relate that places the 1957 experience of Brazilian farmer-turned-lawyer Antonio Villas Boas in a whole new, disturbing light. In the late 1970s, Reynolds had a number of exchanges with an enigmatic, shadowy, and now-deceased Yugoslavian character named Bosco Nedelcovic, who worked for the Department of State's Agency for International Development (AID) in South America, and later with the Department of Defense.

It was during a telephone call in February 1978, Reynolds recalls, when Nedelcovic provided "sketchy details" concerning his, Nedelcovic's, participation in a number of UFO-related "missions" within the borders of South America in the late 1950s. According to Nedelcovic, on one particular occasion in October 1957, he was instructed by his "immediate supervisor" in the AID to report to Aeroporto Santos Dumont in Rio de Janeiro, where he boarded a military transport helicopter, along with two additional AID personnel. A doctor and a Brazilian naval officer were also along for the flight. The crew, meanwhile, was all American, and consisted of a pilot, co-pilot, and navigator.

As Reynolds listened, Nedelcovic continued that the team flew to a "Brazilian/American base" in the Serro do Espinhaco, and subsequently undertook several reconnaissance flights over Pico da Bandeira, the third-highest mountain in Brazil. Reynolds was told: "Various apparatus was tested during the flights but the three men from AID did not participate directly in the testing. They had been briefed on the mission and their function was outlined as auxiliary in nature. The briefing indicated that the men were participating in new forms of psychological testing that would eventually be used in military contexts" (Reynolds, 1978).

Several days later, the team boarded the same helicopter and flew to a base at Espinhaco. This time, one more Navy man was present, as was a whole variety of "electronic gear" that included "an oversized radar scope" and an approximately 3-foot-by-5-foot "chrome-like cubicle." "Medical-gear" was also on board, Nedelcovic advised Reynolds. The helicopter flew on to Uberaba, where it touched down, although no one disembarked. Reynolds states that he was advised the team then "flew the Rio Grande River area and scanned the terrain with the helicopter sweep lights." They then flew back to Uberaba, where they spent the night—in the helicopter (Ibid.).

The next evening, something dramatic occurred: After several hours of flying the same route as the night before, they "hovered over a person below who had been discovered by heat-sensing devices on board" (Ibid.). They descended to a height of approximately 200 feet and released a "chemical derivative" above the man that could result in amnesia, as well as distortion of the senses and motor functions. Shortly after doing so, the pilot landed the helicopter.

The victim, although "groggy," was not immobile and "started to run." It was not a difficult task for the three AID personnel to pursue him, catch up to him, and subdue him, however. Nedelcovic said the man was dragged back to the helicopter and taken aboard—but not before falling face-forward and hitting his lower jaw on the "helicopter ramp-rung" (Ibid.).

Nedelcovic recalled that the man was on board the helicopter for around two hours—a time period throughout which the three AID employees waited outside, on the ground.

Reynolds says that at roughly the two-hour mark, "...the man was passed through the helicopter hatch, at about 3 a.m.; he was unconscious. The other two AID men took him to a tractor that was in the field and laid him next to it" (Ibid.). The helicopter was then flown back to Uberaba, after which they returned to the Espinhaco base, and before Nedelcovic resumed his regular work in Sao Paulo.

Reynolds notes in relation to the incident: "This is, of course, the thoroughly reported and famous Villas Boas case." He adds, quite reasonably: "Anyone could read this account and make up a story like [Nedelcovic's]—even going so far as adding the nice touch about Villas Boas' bang-on-the-jaw, which would account for the marks on Villas Boas' chin that he recounts as 'bloodletting' by the ufonauts that abducted him" (Ibid.).

But does that mean that Nedelcovic did make it all up? Was there any motivation for him to fabricate such a story? If he wasn't merely spinning a tall-tale, does that mean we need to drastically reassess the tale of Antonio Villas Boas—and perhaps other claims of alien contact, too? Could it really have been the case that Villas Boas did not meet Space-Brother-like extraterrestrials from some far-off world, but, instead, had his mind manipulated by rather large and burly men in standard-issue military flight-suits? If so, why? With all those controversial questions swirling around our heads, we should look deeper into the claims of Reynolds's informant.

According to Nedelcovic, the Villas Boas case was not an isolated event. Rather, he maintained to Reynolds, decades ago elements of the CIA and the military were deliberately engaging in the outright fabrication of alien-contact incidents—and were apparently having a lot of success when it came to pulling the wool over the eyes of easy-to-influence witnesses. Reynolds explains that Nedelcovic told him he was assigned to the Department of Defense in 1963, as a translator for the military—a position that took him, unsurprisingly, overseas where "he worked with foreign dignitaries visiting military installations in [the United States]" (Reynolds, 1978).

Reynolds records that Nedelcovic "...was regularly assigned to CIA briefings on UFOs for NATO officers and CIA operatives in Europe,

United States Air Force officers and, occasionally, United States Naval officers participated in the briefings" (Ibid.).

Reynolds's notes on this curious affair reveal that in the 1964–65 time-period Nedelcovic specifically "…took part in briefings that outlined procedures for UFO episodes in England. RAF officers and other British military personnel participated. NATO officers were present, as well as CIA operatives and United States military. Plans were made for 'visual displays, radar displacement, and artifact droppings.' Materials were shipped through the Netherlands Defense NATO depot in New Jersey. Coordination of events was placed within jurisdiction of Lakenheath RAF Station in England" (Ibid.).

Nedelcovic also wanted to talk about a strange and controversial Contactee case that has become known as the Scoriton Mystery. Reynolds outlines the story:

A man named E. Arthur Bryant reported a UFO sighting for April 24th, 1965 in Scoriton, England, the County of Devon, near Dartmoor. Mr. Bryant also noted, in letters to the Exeter Astronomical Society, other sightings. What is fascinating about the Bryant incident is his alleged contact with beings in that 'flying saucer'—one of whom referred to himself as Yamski, apparently a reincarnation of George Adamski who had died only hours before.

The whole, intriguing affair was covered in a book by British UFO investigator Eileen Buckle, *The Scoriton Mystery*, and a booklet by Norman Oliver, *Sequel to Scoriton*. Bryant provided 'technical gear' and avid descriptions of the interiors of the crafts and the beings therein. He also divulged information that was only privy, allegedly, to George Adamski and supplied to him, Bryant, by Yamski and his saucerian colleagues.

Norman Oliver, initially a believer in the Bryant encounter, ended up discounting the whole affair as a hoax, with some Machiavellian elements. Ms. Buckle continued to believe Arthur Bryant and even got an assertion of truth from him as he lay dying in hospital [from the effects of a brain-tumor on] June 24th, 1967. Like all UFO incidents, the Bryant story is filled with interesting, but strange details; some provable as erroneous and others not so easily dismissed (Ibid.).

What about Nedelcovic's views on the Scoriton affair? Reynolds's copious notes tell a fascinating story: "[Nedelcovic] said he remembered the Scoriton incident rather vividly because at a briefing in January 1969 the CIA reported the death of a man in 1968 [Nedelcovic was wrong here: Bryant died in 1967, as noted above] from excessive experimentation. The event was referred to as the '1965 Devonshire episode.' Later on [Nedelcovic] saw reports that also brought attention to the 'microwave incident,' with admonitions to CIA and NSA [National Security Agency] operatives about the injudicious use of microwave technology. He remembers no restraints on drug experimentation. He did not know the name of the person involved in the episode but had seen reports referring to the Scoriton book" (Ibid.).

Reynolds reveals that, according to Nedelcovic, at least, the truth of the matter was as follows: "In the 1964-65 project (called *Exeter* to correspond to comtemporary episodes planned for Exeter, New Hampshire in the United States and Exeter in England) 'sighting' coordinates were established for a triangular area in England that included Dover, Cambridge, Warminster, and Exeter (in Devonshire); because that covered the populous London region and rural countryside.

In one of the sightings of 1965 (which [Nedelcovic] learned about from the 1969 briefing) a man [presumably Bryant] reported a sighting and dropping of material to one of the British UFO groups. CIA operatives on the staff or as members contacted the man about the sighting. While passing the information to Lakenheath through the London CIA office as part of the *Exeter* project, someone decided to subject the witness to further UFO experience (Ibid.).

The man was taken to London where he accepted the offer to have his story verified by the use of a 'truth seeking drug.' During this session a doctor administered experimental drugs used to induce specific hallucinatory material into a subject's brain processes. In this case the man was also stimulated by microwave transmissions so that material induced would be retained upon awakening as if a real events. [Nedelcovic] said he saw reports of many such episodes but this was the only one he remembers as having a death attributed directly to the experiment itself (Ibid.).

In essence, that is Nedelcovic's story as it was told to Reynolds back in 1978. But what is Reynolds's view on the event today? He says: "When I was first in touch with Nedelcovic he was looking for money to finance this kind of hippy commune he was anxious to set up. And, my first thought was that he was trying to ingratiate himself with us so that we might give some money; that he was just feeding us this as a story we would want to hear. But then, when I looked into it, it turned out he was all the things that he said he was."

Reynolds admits: "When I heard [the story] from Nedelcovic for the first time, I thought it was too fantastic: the idea of the government getting hold of Villas Boas and subjecting him to various experimental drugs and a conditioned scenario, to see how he would react. But, now, I'm not sure. I used to think the Contactee stories were just contrivances by a bunch of people who needed attention. I was around in the fifties and I saw those people then as just wanting their fifteen-minutes of fame—long before Andy Warhol came along. But, now, when I look at it from a later perspective, you think: was somebody using them? I think, now, that it's tied in with the government manipulating them" (Reynolds, 2009).

Reynolds is very keen to stress that he does believe there is a genuine UFO phenomenon of undetermined origins, but that has not stopped the official world from ingeniously exploiting that same phenomenon for its own ends: "The evidence is overwhelming that there's a real UFO presence. And, back in the late 40s, and at least to the 60s, I think the government knew something, or had some evidence for, the possibility of a real alien confrontation that might happen. But before it did happen, they were trying to see, and needed to see, what the public's reaction would be: would there be a panic? Would the Russians be able to take advantage of something like that? Before the confrontation happened, the CIA— or whoever—contrived these things with Villas Boas and others. In the context of a military experiment, it might have allowed them to study the public's possible reaction to created events and real events" (Reynolds, 2009).

What of the purported alien woman with whom Villas Boas claimed to have had sex? Reynolds offers his views on this particularly controversial matter: "The story from Nedelcovic was that after Villas Boas had been subjected to various drugs, the part with the woman was literally acted out.

So, there may have been a real woman. But in Villas Boas' case, it could have been manipulation-induced. It gave me visions of the CIA employing people of an Asian-kind of demeanor and look. It's in the realm of possibility that someone was concocting a scenario in that way" (Reynolds, 2009).

Reynolds continues: "I think why this was done with the Contactees in the fifties and sixties was because there were a lot of real UFO events back then—there were a lot of reports from France and Italy of people seeing little dwarfish creatures, for example. I think those were absolutely real events. I don't think those cases were set-up or contrived by the government at all. But the CIA didn't know how things might go from there, with the Italian and French cases and other ones, and how they should deal with it if there might have been an invasion. So, they set people up in a UFO contrivance and studied the witness response, and probably studied the public and the media's response too" (Ibid.).

What of today? Reynolds has an interesting response to that question: "It seems that a lot of the UFO presence today has waned since the 50s and 60s, with the landing cases in Europe and things like that. We just don't really see much like that anymore. And because the UFO presence has waned—and there never was the invasion that the government was worried about in the fifties and sixties—the faked, government contrivance has gone on the back-burner; which is why we aren't getting contrivances like the Villas Boas case today" (Ibid.).

Although UFOlogical true-believers might react with dismay, or outright hostility, at the very idea that one of the subject's most famous cases might have actually been the work of government personnel employing the use of sophisticated drugs, hallucinogenic substances, and stage-managed deceptions, consider the following words direct from the mouth of Villas Boas himself, as they relate to his recollections of the "UFO" he claimed to have been taken aboard.

It was, he said: "…like a large elongated egg…On the upper part of the machine there was something which was revolving at great speed and also giving off a powerful fluorescent reddish light." Then, when the experience was over, said Villas Boas, the craft rose "…slowly into the air until it had reached a height of some 30 to 50 meters…The whirring noise of the air being displaced became much more intense and the revolving dish [that sat atop the object] began to turn at a fearful speed…At that moment, the machine suddenly changed direction, with an abrupt movement, making a louder noise, a sort of 'beat'" (Villas Boas, 1958).

A "large elongated egg"-shaped object, atop of which sat a "dish"-like structure that was "revolving at great speed," and that made a sound described as "a sort of beat," does indeed sound astonishingly like a near-perfect description of the body, fast-spinning rotor-blades, and noise commonly associated with a helicopter. Perhaps aliens did not manifest before Antonio Villas Boas on that long-gone 1957 night. But, if the story as related to Rich Reynolds can be considered valid, then there may have been—and may still be—shadowy figures within the official world that were very keen to have us believe that the young farmer really did experience an encounter of the other-worldly kind. To paraphrase *The X-Files*, in the case of Villas Boas, "the truth" might not have come from "out there" after all. It may have originated right here on Earth—deep in the scheming minds of Pentagon generals and CIA spooks.

21

Space-Brothers vs. Crypto-Brothers

One of the most thought-provoking and alternative theories offered in an attempt to provide an explanation for aspects of the ever-mysterious UFO presence on our world comes from Kansas City–based researcher and author Mac Tonnies. Well-known for his keen ability to think definitively outside of the box when it comes to the study of unexplained phenomena, Tonnies has, for a number of years, been deeply involved in the investigation of the possibility that our alleged alien visitors may actually be nothing of the sort. In reality, Tonnies suspects, they could be even stranger. Tonnies takes very seriously the possibility that a significant portion of the UFO mystery might be explainable via the shadowy, manipulative, and ingeniously deceptive presence of what he has dubbed the cryptoterrestrials.

Rather than originating on far-off worlds, Tonnies carefully theorizes, the cryptoterrestrials are, actually, a very ancient and advanced terrestrial body of people, closely related to the human race, who have lived alongside us in secret—possibly deep underground—for countless millennia. In addition, Tonnies suggests that (a) today, their numbers may well be waning; (b) their science may not be too far ahead of our own—although they would dearly like us to believe they are our infinitely advanced technological masters; (c) to move amongst us, and to operate in our society, they ingeniously pass themselves off as aliens; and (d) they are deeply worried by our hostile ways—hence the reason why they are always so keen to warn us of the perils of nuclear destruction and environmental collapse: they are grudgingly forced to share the planet with us, albeit in a distinctly stealthy and stage-managed fashion.

For those who consider such a scenario to be too fantastic for words, give careful consideration to Tonnies' findings, thoughts, and conclusions on this matter. As you will see, collectively, they may very well hold the key that opens the door to the truth of certain aspects of the Space-Brothers puzzle.

After devouring countless books on the UFO controversy and the paranormal, I began to acknowledge that the extraterrestrial hypothesis suffered [from] some tantalizing flaws. In short, the 'aliens' seemed more like surreal caricatures of ourselves than beings possessing the god-like technology one might plausibly expect from interstellar visitors. Like Jacques Vallee, I came to the realization that the extraterrestrial hypothesis isn't strange enough to encompass the entirety of occupant cases. But if we're dealing with humanoid beings that evolved here on Earth, some of the problems vanish. I envision the cryptoterrestrials engaged in a process of subterfuge, bending our belief systems to their own ends. And I suggest that this has been occurring, in one form or another, for an extraordinarily long time. I think there's a good deal of folkloric and mythological evidence pointing in this direction, and I find it most interesting that so many descriptions of ostensible 'aliens' seem to reflect staged events designed to misdirect witnesses and muddle their perceptions (Tonnies, 2009).

Tonnies also has an opinion on the 1957 case of Antonio Villas Boas; it is an opinion that is very different to the claim of Bosco Nedelcovic. On one point, however, there is a degree of concurrence: Tonnies strongly doubts that Villas Boas met extraterrestrials:

I regard the alleged 'hybridization program' with skepticism. How sure are we that these interlopers are extraterrestrial? It seems more sensible to assume that the so-called aliens are human, at least in some respects. Indeed, descriptions of intercourse with aliens fly in the face of exobiological thought. If the cryptoterrestrial population is genetically impoverished, as I assume it is, then it might rely on a harvest of human genes to augment its dwindling gene-pool. It would be most advantageous to have us believe we're dealing with omnipotent extraterrestrials rather than a fallible sister species. The ET-UFO mythos may be due, in part, to a long-running and most successful disinformation campaign (Ibid.).

Expanding upon this same line of thought, Tonnies adds:

After intercourse, the big-eyed succubus that seduced Antonio Villas-Boas pointed skyward, implying a cosmic origin. But the mere fact that she appeared thoroughly female, and, moreover, attractive, belies an unearthly explanation. Further, one could argue that the clinical environment he encountered aboard the landed 'spacecraft' was deliberately engineered to reinforce his conviction that he was dealing with extraterrestrials. If cryptoterrestrials are using humans to improve their genetic stock, it stands to reason they've seen at least a few of our saucer movies. As consummate anthropologists, they likely know what we expect of 'real' extraterrestrials and can satisfy our preconceptions with a magician's skill. Their desire for our continued survival, if only for the sake of our genetic material, may have played a substantial role in helping us to avoid extinction during the Cold War, when the UFO phenomenon evolved in our skies; much to the consternation of officialdom (Ibid.).

On the matter of the Space-Brothers in general, Tonnies says: Historically, the Contactees have come to be viewed as something of an embarrassment; a frivolous distraction from serious UFO research. I see them as a valuable window on a pivotal era, at least as influential on popular culture as the Beats. To view them in a ufological vacuum is to deliberately overlook the deep archetypal forces simmering just beneath the surface.

Commentators regularly assume that all the Contactees were lying or else delusional. But if we're experiencing a staged reality, some of the beings encountered by the Contactees might have

Mac Tonnies, seeker of the cryptoterrestrials. Photo courtesy of Mac Tonnies.

been real; and the common messages of universal brotherhood could have been a sincere attempt to curb our destructive tendencies. The extraterrestrial guise would have served as a prudent disguise, neatly misdirecting our attention and leading us to ask the wrong questions; which we're still asking with no substantial results (Ibid.).

No one, having by now digested countless tales of a definitively Contactee-nature, can deny Tonnies' observations when he notes: "Contactees and abductees alike describe the interiors of 'alien' vehicles in curiously cinematic terms. The insides of presumed spaceships often seem like lavish props from never-filmed sci-fi dramas. The aliens don't fare any better; they behave like jesters, dutifully regurgitating fears of ecological blight and nuclear war but casually inserting allusions that seem more in keeping with disinformation than genuine ET revelations" (Ibid.).

Tonnies admits:

The cryptoterrestrial hypothesis has met with mixed reactions. Some [UFO researchers] seem to think I'm onto something. Most UFO researchers are, at best, extremely skeptical. Others think

I'm parroting John Keel's 'superspectrum,' a variation on the 'parallel worlds' theme that in turn shares memes with Jacques Vallee's 'multiverse.' Both ideas suggest that we somehow occupy dimensional space with our 'alien' visitors, doing away with the need for extraterrestrial spacecraft while helping explain the sense of absurdity that accompanies many UFO and occupant sightings. Keel and Vallee have both ventured essentially 'occult' ideas in cosmological terms; both the 'superspectrum' and the 'multiverse' require a revision of our understanding of the way reality itself works. But the cryptoterrestrial hypothesis is grounded in a more familiar context.

I'm not suggesting unseen dimensions or the need for ufonauts to 'downshift' to our level our consciousness. Rather, I'm asking if it's feasible that the alleged aliens that occupy historical and contemporary mythology are flesh-and-blood human-like creatures that live right here on Earth. Not another version of Earth in some parallel Cosmos, but our Earth. While I can't automatically exclude the UFO phenomenon's 'paranormal' aspects, I can attempt to explain them in technological terms. For example, I see no damning theoretical reason why 'telepathy' and 'dematerialization' can't ultimately be explained by appealing to cybernetics, nanotechnology and other fields generally excluded from ufological discourse (Ibid.).

Tonnies notes with some irony: "The cryptoterrestrial hypothesis manages to alienate champions of the extraterrestrial hypothesis and those who support a more esoteric, 'inter-dimensional' explanation. It offers no clear-cut reconciliation. It does, however, wield explanatory potential lacking in both camps" (Ibid.).

Before you consider writing off Tonnies's words, it is important to note that they do not stand alone. For example, writer-researcher E.A. Guest has made a valuable contribution to this particular issue. Guest's father served in the U.S. Air Force in the late 1950s, and his work exposed him to issues relating to "training pilots in altitude chambers," the U.S. space-program, "flight medicine training," and much more (Guest, 2005). Significantly, during the period of his employment with the military, Guest's father received at Wright-Patterson Air Force Base, Ohio, a secret briefing relative to the famous story of the UFO crash at Roswell, New Mexico in the summer of 1947.

Guest says that by the time of his father's briefing, the Air Force had come to a startling conclusion: Neither the strange aerial device nor the bodies found in the desert outside of Roswell at the time in question had alien origins. Rather, says Guest, "According to my father, these vehicles came from inside the planet. The civilization…exists in a vast, underground system of caverns and tunnels beneath the southwest and is human. They went underground thousands of years ago" (Guest, 2005).

Guest was additionally told by his father that: "Occasionally, they come and go, emerging in their vehicles, and occasionally they crash. They are human in appearance, so much so that they can move among us with ease with just a little effort. If you get a close look, you'd notice something odd, but not if the person just passed you on the street" (Guest, 2005). Interestingly, echoing Tonnies's words about how the cryptoterrestrials may have actually created the ruse that they are aliens to hide their true identity, Guest says: "I believe that the ET hypothesis has been used by the 'aliens' themselves, because it is most readily embraced by people who have had encounters with them" (Guest, 2005).

Consider, too, the following from Timothy Green Beckley—whose involvement within the Ufological arena dates back decades—which fits very nicely within the theories of Tonnies: "One of the things about the Space-Brothers is that they were certainly deceptive about their point of origin. I don't believe they came from Venus or Mars. Whoever they were, they didn't want people to know where they came from. However, I don't think their overall message was deceptive—of love and light, and wanting us to give up our nuclear weapons.

Some people might suggest that because the Space-Brothers look so much like us that they could be from somewhere right here on Earth—an ancient race, maybe. There are a lot of cultural legends about advanced beings living underground: UFOs coming out of the oceans, lakes, caverns. The whole hollow-Earth thing is a little hard for me; but the cavern theories I can take.

I remember one incident where I was lecturing and a gentleman—a professor at the college where I was lecturing—came up to me and told this story about how he was driving outside of a town in Michigan. It was rather late at night, and he saw these lights in the woods. He pulled over, and there was no other traffic coming in either direction; but there was already another car parked at the side of the road.

He described seeing some sort of ship in the distance—a UFO. A group of human-like aliens got out, walked to the car—which was a Cadillac, or something like that. He watched them and could see they looked human. They just got in the car and drove off. But then, a couple of weeks later, he sees one of the same guys in a supermarket. These reports sound far-fetched; but there's so many of them of what seem to be aliens being able to move among us. But, if they're really from here, that might explain it (Beckley, 2009).

Although the image that all of the above provokes is one suggesting the cryptoterrestrials have been highly successful, in terms of masking the nature of their real, down-to-earth origins, they are not infallible. The very fact that Mac Tonnies believes he may very well be hot on their trail leads him to state: "It's a formidable disguise; but it can be pierced" (Tonnies, 2009).

22

Ghost-Lights

Having now digested a wealth of data on not just the Contactees and their myriad claims of extraterrestrial interaction but also a number of theories that may offer some answers with respect to what lies at the heart of at least some of their assertions, one might be tempted to ask: What else could be said on this particular issue? Well, the answer to that question is quite a lot, actually.

I have saved until now the examination and dissection of a phenomenon that may possibly be the most important of all when it comes to trying to resolve the puzzle of who or what the long-haired and elusive ones really were and, albeit to a lesser degree today, are still. A common factor among many of the Contactee encounters is that they involved direct interaction with unidentified aerial balls of light that were seen in close proximity to the witnesses—phenomena that have become known within Fortean research circles as Ghost-Lights.

Consider the evidence: In March 1950, Samuel Eaton Thompson maintained he underwent a truly bizarre—yet definitively Contactee-driven—encounter in Washington State. Yet, for all of Thompson's detailed claims of lengthy contact with the alleged alien entities, the only evidence he was able to produce from his experience was inconclusive photographs that displayed mere "blobs of light" (*Centralia Daily Chronicle*, 1950). Daniel Fry's experience at White Sands began after he caught sight of what he interpreted as an "especially bright group of stars" that "seemed to beckon me" (Fry, 1992).

Several of Truman Bethurum's interactions with Captain Aura Rhanes followed directly on from Bethurum having viewed what he perceived as "a meteor falling through the starlit purple night," or in the wake of his having encountered what he described as "a small flare" (Bethurum, 1970).

Then there was experience of Orfeo Angelucci, which commenced with his sighting of a red, glowing, oval-shaped light that was "about five times as large as the red portion of a traffic light" (Angelucci, 2008). Angelucci noted that, as the red-colored ball departed at a fast rate of speed, a pair of smaller, fluorescent green objects, each about 3-feet in diameter, flew out of it and headed in Angelucci's direction. They hung several feet above his car for a few minutes, after which something very strange and profound occurred.

Emanating from between the two green balls of light, said Angelucci, was the sound of "a masculine voice in strong, well-modulated tones and speaking perfect English." Stressing that he should not be scared, the voice told Angelucci that he was in direct communication with "friends from another world" (Ibid.).

Then, from within the lights, there appeared a screen, in which Angelucci could see the heads and shoulders of a man and a woman ("as though in a cinema close-up") who he described as being "the ultimate of perfection." Their faces took on beaming smiles as they began to engage Angelucci in telepathic conversation and as "new comprehensions that would have required hours of conversation to transmit" filled the mind of Angelucci (Ibid.).

Remember, too, that Angelucci's mysterious confidante, Adam, said that his first experience followed his sighting of a "wayward star" that proceeded to take on the appearance of a flying saucer (Ibid.).

Similarly, Dana Howard said of one of her most profound encounters: "I saw a rising glow of phosphorescence. It was very tall at first, but out of this phosphorescent substance a form began to manifest…a solid, fleshy being, delicate in charm and manner" (Lee, 2007).

When Ralph Lael allegedly encountered unidentified phenomena on Brown Mountain, North Carolina in the late 1950s, he stated that he was witness to several unidentified floating lights, 10-to-12-feet across, that had "three feelers" protruding from them. As one of the lights approached him, Lael recorded that, in his opinion, "…it was alive and had intelligence" (Lael, 1965).

Take note, too, of the words of Tim Beckley, who personally met with Lael in the 1960s:

Ralph was certainly a character—one of the lesser-known Contactees. People like Adamski and Van Tassel are well known. But, there are hundreds, maybe thousands, of individuals, like Ralph, who claim they have had encounters with golden-haired aliens, flown to other planets, and been given messages. John Keel called them 'Silent Contactees'—the less-well-known Contactees whose stories hardly ever got talked about. And Ralph was definitely one of these.

When I spoke to Ralph back in the 60s, he seemed sincere. Those Brown Mountain Lights must have had some effect on him. There were some strange stories going on out there with the lights, and there were other people who claimed to have come close to them. The lights did seem intelligent; and they may have had a mesmerizing and hypnotic effect on people (Beckley, 2009).

Echoing much of the data contained in this chapter, Beckley makes the following observation:

Maybe there is some energy upon the Earth that is trying to have some information come out; or some philosophy come out. I would uphold that theory if we were talking about the UFO beings, or Mormonism, or Christianity. The literal physical experience: we maybe take it with a grain of salt; but it's more of the spiritual intention of the philosophy behind the story that matters. So, were the Contactees story-tellers? Yes. But, they were story-tellers with a legitimate message that came from somewhere (Ibid.).

Matthew Williams, Crop Circle Authority. Courtesy of Nick Redfern.

Bob Short, one of the last surviving, original Contactees, has described his awareness of three distinct types of UFOs: one that has the appearance of a "disk;" one that is "cigar"-shaped; and a third that he calls "luminous ephemeral spheres of light." Short may have hit the nail on the head when he says that these luminous spheres are "so dazzling" that "…the actual form behind the light is masked and cannot be scrutinized visually" (Short, 2003).

It should also be noted that sightings of unidentified flying balls of light have been associated with Crop Circles—a subject which has a deep link to the Space-Brother issue. Matthew Williams is a long-time student of the Crop Circle puzzle who has also engaged in the construction of complex formations in the fields of England. But Williams is no hoaxer. Rather, he is convinced his actions are guided by a higher form of intelligence. But what might be the nature of the intelligence by which Williams claims to be guided? As the following words from the man himself demonstrate, the intelligence may well be—just as was the case with the Contactees of decades past—Ghost-Light-like in nature:

There was one time, I'd rather not say when or where exactly, as I could get into trouble for admitting I trespassed on the farmer's land and made the formation. Plus, I had a friend named Paul helping me with this one. We were making this circle when we noticed these three bright lights—small balls of lights coming towards the field. We watched them; we were fascinated. But they split up and each of them went to a corner of the field—and which only left one corner for us to leave by without getting too close to these things. That was a bit unsettling. We didn't know what these balls were; so we raced out of the open corner of the field. We looked back as we ran and could see the balls heading towards us: gliding very gracefully just above the top of the crop. It was like they were on a railway track, just moving very smoothly, but it left us sort of disturbed too: like they were almost ghostly and alive (Williams, 2006).

Quite clearly, there is a pattern at work here: In all of the Contactee cases cited above, the encounters were associated with, or began with, the sighting of flying—or floating—balls of light that seemed to exhibit a degree of intelligence, and that then transformed into either gleaming flying saucers, or benevolent extraterrestrials that engaged the shell-shocked witnesses in one-to-one conversation, and demanded some form of specific task of them—such as informing the world of the dangers of atomic weaponry.

In relation to the testimony of Matthew Williams: Even though he most certainly does not consider himself to be a Contactee of the type that the term has typified since the 1950s, the fact that Williams has experienced close encounters with aerial balls of light in Crop Circles of his own making should not be ignored. Moreover, as noted above, Williams openly states that he feels he is being used by higher, advanced intelligences to construct such formations—formations that have had life-altering effects upon the thousands of people who have flocked to see them, walk within them, and investigate them, such as Vanessa Martin.

In view of the above, could it be that the Ghost-Lights are the actual root cause of such encounters; as well as being the root cause of those same altered states, too? Might the Ghost-Lights be actual, living, sentient beings? If so, do the Ghost-Lights have the ability to control our minds to the extent that they can make us believe we are seeing wise, blond-haired Venusians, when, in actuality, something radically different in both origin and appearance is carefully manipulating and stage-managing the entire experience? Could it be that the actions of the Ghost-Lights are prompted by a deep yearning for contact with other intelligent entities—the human race—for reasons relative to manipulation, and for provoking radical change and transformation at both an individual and a collective level? Though such questions and scenarios may seem outrageous, the answers to all of those same questions could well be in the affirmative.

In May 2006, it was announced that after decades of secretly investigating UFOs, the British Ministry of Defense had finally come to the conclusion that aliens were not visiting our planet. The MoD's assertions were revealed within the pages of a formerly classified document that had been commissioned in 1996, and that was completed in February 2000. Titled the *Condign Report*, the 465-page document demonstrated how British air defense experts had decided that UFO sightings were the result of "natural but relatively rare and not completely understood phenomena"—such as plasmas (*Flying Saucery Presents…The Real UFO Project*, 2009).

UFO researchers Dr. David Clarke and Gary Anthony—who were at the forefront of the effort to get the MoD to declassify the *Condign Report*—noted the following in relation to the secret study:

> Mr. X [the title given by Clarke and Anthony to the still-unidentified MoD-sponsored author] goes even further by drawing upon the controversial research and conclusions of research carried out at Laurentian University by Michael Persinger. He finds merit in the theory that plasmas or earthlights may explain a range of close-encounter and even 'alien abduction' experiences. The report says that on rare occasions plasmas can cause responses in the temporal-lobe area of the human brain, leading observers to suffer extended memory retention and repeat experiences. This, the report's author believes, may be 'a key factor in influencing the more extreme reports [that] are clearly believed by the victims' (Clarke, 2006).

Dr. Greg Little, commenting on such unidentified balls of light, says: "Persinger's primary interest has been in the nearly unbelievable effects the plasma's magnetic field has on human consciousness…Persinger's research indicates that people who come into close contact with these charged plasma forms experience altered states of consciousness producing a host of strange visions: UFO abductions, apparitional phenomena, sightings of improbable creatures (e.g., Bigfoot), fairies, and alien-like creatures" (Little, 2003).

What, exactly, is the temporal lobe that Persinger believes may play a significant role in such matters? Essentially, it is a region of the cerebral cortex that is found beneath the Sylvian fissure on both the left and right hemispheres of the brain, and that is involved in auditory processing. In addition, the temporal lobe plays an important role in the processing of semantics in both speech and vision, as well as in the formation of long-term memory, and its transference from the short-term memory state. In other words, the temporal lobe is a vital component of the process by which we interpret and compartmentalize audio-visual phenomena, and plays a significant role in the way in which we recall such phenomena, via our memories.

Of course, an advanced intelligence having the ability to influence, or outright manipulate, such a complex tool as the temporal lobe might well possess the ability to make us see, hear, and later recall just about anything it wanted—such as, perhaps, a long-haired alien claiming to come from some far-off world. But is such a theory really feasible?

British researcher Paul Devereux—who is a recognized authority on Ghost-Light phenomena—says that a not-fully understood by-product of stresses and strains in the Earth's crust may indeed produce such Ghost-Light-type plasmas; however, in other instances, he offers, there is an intriguing possibility that the Ghost-Lights may very well represent a type of literal life-form. Devereux notes that, if such reports can be considered credible, then at least some of the lights may be demonstrating a "playful, animal-like curiosity" (Devereux, 2007).

Expanding on this issue, he adds: "But this is a forbidden topic. For one thing, it raises the tricky question of the nature of consciousness…To even suggest that consciousness might manifest in geophysical contexts as well as biological ones is to go beyond the pale" (Ibid.).

What if the British Ministry of Defense is at least partially correct, and this "not completely understood phenomena" is indeed responsible for claims of alien encounters via its affect on the temporal lobe? But what if the MoD is wrong in its conclusion that this same phenomenon and its subsequent affect on the mind is a wholly natural one? What if the "playful, animal-like curiosity" shown by some Ghost-Lights of the type that Paul Devereux has commented upon is evidence that they are sentient beings in their own unique right?

If the natural state of existence of these intelligences is in the form of balls of light, and if they do possess high levels of intelligence—rather than just rudimentary degrees of self-awareness—is it not possible or conceivable that they might deliberately and consciously affect the human temporal-lobe area to induce Contactee-style accounts—as a means of having some form of one-to-one communication with us, and in a fashion that we can at least begin to understand, to which we can relate, and that might even enlighten and transform us?

If so, perhaps when the Contactee movement was in its formative years, the Ghost-Lights were picking up on humankind's cultural beliefs concerning aliens, as well as its fears of Cold War confrontation and atomic destruction. Maybe they were manifesting—albeit purely inwardly to the participant—in a guise that might very well have been both expected and welcome in the 1950s: namely that of reassuring, human-like, blond-haired aliens visiting from a nearby planet such as Venus. Don't forget that Ralph Lael's encounter on Brown Mountain, North Carolina—that had tales of ancient atomic destruction at its very heart—occurred at the same time as the Cuban Missile Crisis came perilously close to spiraling out of control. That the serious nature of the Cuban events may well have been dominating Lael's mind is very understandable. And this may explain why the "aliens" that appeared before him offered thoughts and scenarios pertaining to nuclear war: the phenomenon was picking up on Lael's own internal worries that the human race was on the verge of exterminating itself.

Maybe that is why, in centuries past, fairy encounters were often reported in association with small balls of light. When there was an acceptance that fairies were literally real entities, perhaps the intelligences behind the ghostly lights tapped into the beliefs of the time, and subsequently manipulated the subconscious of the witnesses to ensure that a meeting of minds occurred in a fashion that was acceptable to their particular, now-centuries-old and largely defunct and forgotten cultural beliefs.

Make no mistake: Such historical fairy-based cases, that are associated with aerial balls of light, abound. Consider the following story from 1910, recorded one year later by W.Y. Evans-Wentz, a renowned expert on Celtic beliefs, mythologies, and legends relative to the world of fairies, and which is practically identical in nature to the initial stages of the famous encounter of Orfeo Angelucci. In fact, so similar is the tale told to Evans-Wentz (by one of "my fellow students in Oxford, a native Irishman of County Kerry"), one is almost forced to accept the notion that the phenomenon that appeared before Angelucci in 1950s California was also engaged in a bit of night time prowling around the villages of Ireland some 40 years earlier.

Evans-Wentz's source related the details of the experience as follows:

Some few weeks before Christmas, 1910, at midnight on a very dark night, I and another young man—who like myself was then about twenty-three years of age—were on horseback on our way home from Limerick. When near Listowel, we noticed a light about half a mile ahead. At first it seemed to be no more than a light in some house; but as we came nearer to it and it was passing out of our direct line of vision we saw that it was moving up and down, to and fro, diminishing to a spark, then expanding into a yellow luminous flame. Before we came to Listowel we noticed two lights, about one hundred yards to our right, resembling the light seen first.

Suddenly each of these lights expanded into the same sort of yellow luminous flame, about six feet high by four feet broad. In the midst of each flame we saw a radiant being having human form. Presently the lights moved toward one another and made contact, whereupon the two beings in them were seen to be walking side by side. The beings' bodies were formed of a pure dazzling radiance of the sun, and much brighter than they yellow light or aura surrounding them.

So dazzling was the radiance, like a halo, round their heads that we could not distinguish the countenances of the beings; though their heads were very clearly outlined because this halo-like radiance, which was the brightest light about them, seemed to radiate from or rest upon the head of each being. As we traveled on, a house intervened between us and the lights, and we saw no more of them. It was the first time we had ever seen such phenomena, and in our hurry to get home we were not wise enough to stop and make further examination" (Evans-Wentz, 2004). Notably, just as was the case with Angelucci, this particular encounter was a precursor to yet further supposed other-worldly events in the life of the witness: "...ever since that night I have frequently seen, both in Ireland and in England, similar lights with spiritual beings in them" (Angelucci, 2008).

And also just like Angelucci and the rest of the Contactees, Evans-Wentz's source began to develop specific beliefs about the nature of the intelligences he believed had made their presence known to him:

> In whatever country we may be, I believe that we are forever immersed in the spiritual world; but most of us cannot perceive it on account of the unrefined nature of our physical bodies. Through meditation [also utilized by George Van Tassel just prior to his initial night-time encounter at Giant Rock in March 1953] and psychical training one can come to see the spiritual world and its beings.

> We pass into the spirit realm at death and come back into the human world at birth; and we continue to reincarnate [a process that Angelucci's alleged alien contacts told him was a reality] until we have overcome all Earthly desires and mortal appetites. Then the higher life is open to our consciousness and we cease to be human; we become divine beings (Evans-Wentz, 2004).

Still on the matter of fairies, let us briefly return to the controversial 1957 case of Antonio Villas Boas. It will be recalled that, before his departure from the craft to which he was taken, Villas Boas attempted to steal a clock-like device—but was thwarted from doing so by an irate crew member. Researcher Jacques Vallee has noted that Villas Boas described the clock as having one hand and several marks, that would correspond to the 3, 6, 9, and 12 figures of an ordinary clock. However, while time certainly passed by, the clock hand did not.

"The symbolism in this remark by Villas-Boas is clear," says Vallee. "We are reminded of the fairy tales...of the country where time does not pass" (Vallee, 1970). In addition, centuries-old folklore is replete with tales of people who claimed to have visited the realm of the fairies and who tried

to bring back with them a souvenir, only to be thwarted, in one form or another, from doing so at the last minute—just like Villas Boas was.

This is also very similar to Orfeo Angelucci's assertions that after his memorable flight in a flying saucer, he took from the craft a "strange, shining bit of metal." But, just like the material evidence that visitors to the fairy domain tried to bring back to our world in centuries-past, Angelucci's priceless piece of metal "dissipated into nothingness" (Angelucci, 2008).

Mysterious balls of light known as Orbs were photographed at George Van Tassel's Integratron in 2008. Photo courtesy of Nick Redfern.

Interestingly, although, today, the classic imagery provoked by the mere mention of the word "fairy" is of small, fragile creatures possessed of tiny insect-like wings, they were originally depicted as being very different—and, in some cases, appeared in the guise of tall, radiant and angelic-like entities. Not unlike the classic description of the Space-Brothers, one might justifiably say.

On the relationship between the Contactee issue and that of the spirit world—which arguably absolutely dominated the experiences of both George Van Tassel and George Hunt Williamson, as well as that of the witness to events in Ireland in 1910—long-time paranormal authority Brad Steiger says: "In 1963, when I first began seriously investigating the claims of the UFO contactees…I drew immediate parallels between those who channeled Outer Space beings and the spirit mediums who provided inspirational messages from their guides" (Steiger, 2009).

He continues: "…And when many of the contactees told me that the UFOnaut had appeared to them in a 'light and vaporous form' because of the different frequencies between our dimensions, I was again reminded of the 'light and vaporous forms' that had long been associated with the séance room and the spirit circle" (Ibid.).

Steiger adds: "…In my opinion, the phenomenon of the Space Brothers has absolutely nothing to do with the question of whether extraterrestrial intelligence has visited Earth." Moreover, Steiger voices his belief that there is an "external intelligence that has interacted with our species since our creation on this planet…I am also convinced that some kind of symbiotic relationship exists between us and this intelligence. In some way, they need us as much as we need them" (Ibid.).

What of the possibility, as discussed earlier, that such a phenomenon might be able to significantly manipulate the hypnagogic state to induce startling visual imagery, sounds, and much more in the minds the witness— possibly as a means of control and manipulation, as well as carefully camouflaging its real appearance in the process? Certainly, research has been undertaken demonstrating that deliberately inducing hypnagogia is not an impossible task.

The Dream-Machine (or dreamachine) is a stroboscopic flickering device that can produce startling visual stimuli and which was the brainchild of artist Brion Gysin and Beat-author William Burroughs's "systems adviser," Ian Sommerville. Essentially, the device is constructed from a cylinder with slits cut in the sides, and that is placed on a record turntable and rotated at 78 or 45 revolutions per minute. A light-bulb is suspended in the center of the cylinder, and the rotation speed allows the light to escape from the slits at a constant, regular frequency, of between eight and 13 pulses per second. This frequency-range corresponds to alpha-waves: the electrical oscillations that are generally present in the human brain while in a relaxed state.

Studies of those who have used Dream-Machines suggest the pulsating light stimulates the optic nerve and alters the brain's electrical oscillations—to the extent that increasingly bright, complex patterns of color begin to form behind their closed eyelids. Invariably, those same patterns turn into symbols and shapes that both capture and transfix the "viewer." In a number of cases, such actions have resulted in the participant suddenly entering into a state of hypnagogia. If such a condition can be achieved via the use of mere light-bulbs and turntables, then the idea that a far more advanced phenomenon—but one that is also definitively light-dominated in nature—could achieve something very similar seems not so strange or unbelievable.

Perhaps we have evidence of this.

Dr. Leo Sprinkle, who was deeply involved in the investigation of the December 1967 experience of patrolman Herbert Schirmer, said: "Sgt. Schmirer…claimed that he often experienced a 'ringing,' 'numbness,' 'buzzing' in his ears before going to sleep (around 1:30 a.m. or 2:00 a.m.): he believed he had experienced precognitive dreams…he said he felt concern and 'hurt' since the UFO sighting; he described disturbances in his sleep, including incidents in which he awoke and found that he was 'choking' his wife and handcuffing his wife's ankle and wrist; he said that his wife sometimes woke up during the night and placed his gun elsewhere so that it was not in his boots beside his bed where he had been keeping it" (Randle, 2008).

Of course, sleep disturbances (sometimes of a violent, graphic, and disturbing nature) and hearing unusual sounds—such as "buzzing"-type noises—at the moment of sleep, or upon waking, are classic facets of hypnagogia. In view of this, the notion should not be dismissed that Schirmer's experience was purely an internal one, and one that was provoked, controlled, and dictated by intelligences that had the ability to influence those people particularly susceptible to hypnagogia, as Schirmer appears to have been.

Moving on, let us return to the research of Micah Hanks, who says of the possibility that the Brown Mountain Lights may be self-aware entities: "Some people have claimed what seems to be intelligent interaction with the lights. One woman named Cindy—about a mile away from Wiseman's View—told me she has encountered brilliant balls about the size of a small car that drifted over. One night, with a group of people, one of the lights approached and they all waved. She said they all felt like they were being told to say 'Cheese.' It was like they were being watched. They all felt this clear, mental connection. Most people do seem to have a profound, mental experience with the lights. That, to me, is certainly a subjective thing to each individual who sees the lights. When you witness a brilliant, glowing ball of light that could, for all you know, be a UFO, you might report a very life-changing, moving experience" (Hanks, 2009).

Hanks says of the Space-Brother issue:

I think it's fascinating that in most cases of Contactees, if there is something that can be derived from a moving experience that's indicative of contact, or of a presence, or a type of telepathic link or communication with a higher-power, they are going to create that in their own mind.

When I say that, I don't think that everyone who has claimed to have met with, or had an interaction with, presumed aliens is deliberately making it all up in their own minds. I think there's enough evidence to suggest clearly that the Brown Mountain Lights are a very natural, Earth-bound phenomenon. And that being the case, people who interpret the lights from their own cultural perspective and beliefs about UFOs are going to have their worldview shaken. But, what's more interesting and significant is how the mind then deals with being shaken up: it interprets the things to the benefit of the beholder. I think that is what has happened at Brown Mountain with cases like Ralph Lael's.

There's also the thing that maybe back in the fifties, people were a lot more impressionable. Let's say these lights are extraterrestrial, or anomalous, at least, and people have encountered them and interacted with them. The phenomenon, if it has some sort of intelligence, may have used elements of deception to cause the Contactee to feel the experience was something more—or even something less—than what actually occurred (Hanks, 2009).

It seems the Ghost-Lights are not going away anytime soon: Their relationship to the world of the Contactees is still ever-present. In early 2008, I spent a weekend at George Van Tassel's Integratron—where I was lecturing on the subject of how and why the FBI was so concerned by, and interested in, the cosmic claims of Van Tassel and Adamski. While there, I took a number of photographs in the upper chamber of the Integratron, several of which displayed clear and graphic imagery of countless, small floating balls of light.

In research circles, such small illuminated spheres, captured on film, have become known as Orbs. Of course, a purely down-to-earth explanation for such a phenomenon has been offered: It is called backscatter. As a result of the size limitations of today's compact and ultra-compact cameras—and especially digital cameras—the distance between the lens and the built-in flash has decreased, thereby decreasing the angle of light-reflection to the lens, and, as a consequence, increasing the likelihood of light reflection off of normally sub-visible particles, such as dust, pollen, or water droplets. Hence, Orbs can often be seen on such cameras. But not everyone is convinced that all Orbs can be explained away so easily.

Joshua P. Warren, a respected author and investigator of high-strangeness, says:

> There seems to be some kind of association between Orb-like anomalies and paranormal activity beyond our current understanding. One possible tantalizing clue as to the meaning of Orbs may involve findings of the Cuza University in Romania.
>
> In 2003, physicist Mircea Sanduloviciu and his colleagues made a startling announcement. By replicating conditions believed to exist on our infant planet, they created 'blobs' of plasma that seemed to be alive. They constructed a chamber of argon gas in a plasma state then introduced powerful arcs of electricity, representing lightning storms. Cell-like spheres of plasma were spontaneously created in less than a second. The spheres had an outer layer of negatively charged ions, forming clear boundaries. These spheres could grow, replicate by dividing, and even 'communicate.' Such communication was the result of a sphere emanating electromagnetic energy, causing others nearby to vibrate at the same resonance. Sanduloviciu believes these may have been the first forms of life on our planet. 'The emergence of such spheres seems likely to be a prerequisite for biochemical evolution,' he said"
(Warren, 2006).

Warren asks the question: "Could these simple, plasma life forms be the same as Orbs? Perhaps they exist due to, or are created by, the intense energy expended during paranormal manifestations. Of the many theories offered to explain Orbs, this one could be the most insightful" (Ibid.).

If, as Mircea Sanduloviciu believes, such plasmas are very ancient indeed—and may well have even been the first forms of life to exist on our planet—then that would suggest they have always been with us, always manifesting, always playing their mind games, and forever changing their appearance in response to the way in which our own beliefs concerning higher-beings alter and develop. If they were indeed the first life-forms on our world, maybe—before the human race came along—they spent countless eons dreadfully alone, yearning and longing for communication with other intelligent life-forms.

Maybe the Ghost-Lights are the real aliens, and the blonds were merely brain-borne images and hallucinations of their design and making—images and hallucinations specifically created and instilled via manipulation of the temporal lobe and the hypnagogic state to allow for a kind of one-on-one meeting on relatively common ground that would otherwise have been completely incomprehensible to the mind of humankind.

And don't forget the words of Brad Steiger that may have a direct bearing upon the above theorizing: "…some kind of symbiotic relationship exists between us and this intelligence. In some way, they need us as much as we need them" (Steiger, 2009).

Conclusions

In view of the data imparted in the previous chapter, if you are ever lucky enough to see such a Ghost-Light, from which miraculously appears a benevolent Space-Brother with a flowing head of luxuriant blonde hair, don't run from it, and don't ignore it. But don't necessarily accept the encounter at a literal level either. Instead, always remember that you may be dealing with something akin to Vanessa Martin's Heyoka trickster, or a terribly alone Ghost-Light. Just open your mind, embrace the experience, and see what happens. In its own unique way, the phenomenon may just want to say "Hi"—and perhaps even enlighten and radically transform you at an individual level, too. Just as it may have done to Joseph Smith on that fateful night in 1827; in the villages of Ireland in 1910; and, of course to Adamski, Van Tassel, Bethurum, Angelucci, Lael, Howard, and all the rest of that unique and largely-long-gone band that will forever be known as the Contactees.

Colin Bennett makes an astute observation on this matter: "Many Orthons have appeared throughout history. The equivalents to Adamski's Venusian 'space brother' have appeared on mountain tops, in deserts, and have appeared to walk on water, or fly in the sky. Their sole function is to sow seeds in the head; just as a farmer grows a particular crop. These seeds act on the imagination, which replicates and amplifies whatever story-technology is around at the time. People such as Adamski and the rest of the Contactees were, and still are, like psychic lightning—rods for certain brands of information" (Bennett, 2009).

Bennett clearly recognizes the deceptive nature of the phenomenon when he says: "…we must be careful here. As the alchemist said to his apprentice, 'the game may be rigged, but it's the only game in town'" (Ibid.).

Bennett makes an important point that expands upon his above-statement: "Deception and all its ramifications is the key to this whole business. This does not burst the bubble of the mystery, however; for manipulative levels of faction may well be our first clue as to how a possible alien mind might work. If the levels of deception of all kinds in human culture are anything to go by, [then] the range of such within an alien culture must be both multiple and profound" (Ibid.).

He states further:

The 'space-folk' are sculptured by wars between rival viral memes competing for prime-time belief. It may be that, as an independent form of non-organic life, memes as active viral information can display an Orthon entity at a drop of a hat. [They] come complete with sets of cultural agendas. After they have rung the doorbell as it were, and the goods are sold, these metaphysical salesmen disappear like the traditional Men in Black, no doubt traveling on to seed other dreams in other towns and other heads. The goods we have unwittingly bought are half-formed memories of having met someone from another world.

Over a half-century later, we can no more erase the legendary Contactees from our heads than we can erase Elvis Presley or Marilyn Monroe. Once induced by mere transient suggestion, these powerful images become permanent fast-breeders, turning out scripts and performances in all our heads—for no-one can escape—even as we sleep.

It might come as a disappointment to extraterrestrial nut-and-bolters, but as [Jacques] Vallee says in *Passport to Magonia*, Orthon and his brood may be a form of 'alien' life that has been with us for a long time. Such ethereal beings are part of the structure of that much-despised and rather unfashionable idea described by the phrase mystical experience (Ibid.).

Bennett elaborates further:

A man says he has seen a fairy being. Another man says that is impossible, because fairy beings do not exist. When we subtract the two beliefs we do not get zero as an answer. We have the thinnest of belief-tissue remaining, but perhaps mechanical quantity is irrelevant. The smallest part of an HTML address contains the whole address, rather like a fractal.

These creatures, though seen and photographed, leave no trace of fights, no food swath, no blood, [and] no sweat. [They] appear as partially-formed displays rather than flesh and blood as we know it. It is somewhat chilling to think that if an Orthon or even, perhaps, a Jesus can appear in this manner, then so can many things else, including objects and even situations. In this, it is possible that we are host-receptors of skunk-smoke from life forms not yet known to us.

There is no doubt that Contactee claims allow access to a refreshing world which includes humor, and inspired absurdity. They allow humanity to breathe and access a *Matrix* world in which anything that can be imagined can happen. It might be denied by social-scientific left, but the truth is that dreams, fantasies, and mystical experiences of all kinds play an absolutely essential part in all human mental operations.

George Adamski played a significant part in establishing New Age thinking. It might be well to remember that the entire body of our moral philosophy and spiritual life is formed by visions and inspirations. It does not come from science or technology. Those who thoughtlessly dismiss mystical experience cut themselves off from all art, literature, and no small part of all thought and philosophy. As mystics and prophets know, when desert light strikes the retina, anything that can be imagined can happen. The greatest tribute that can be paid to Adamski is that through both foul means and fair, he helped to create one of the very few routes to the unconscious that we have (Ibid.).

Bennett concludes, with much justification: "Maybe the aliens, as psychic goods, are perpetually under construction' (Ibid.).

The final word goes to the always-insightful Greg Bishop:

> In my opinion, there is a non-human intelligence that interacts with the Human Race, and that has done since whenever; maybe it's always been here—as long as us. I think that actually is true.

> When you see something that your mind doesn't understand and has nowhere to put it, it's going to find a way to do both. And if that involves a three-dimensional here-and-now, knock-on-metal type of craft, aliens with blond hair who look just like us, or bug-eyed aliens, I think your mind is going to form around that. Then it's going to make a decision and a conclusion about what you're dealing with (Bishop, 2009).

> There are probably Contactees who will get mad at me for saying that. But I'm not saying something doesn't happen to them. I'm saying that what happens is controlled by whatever the outside intelligence is that's doing it; and it's not only stranger than we think: it's stranger than we can think. I think whatever the intelligence is it can make us believe whatever it wants—which is what it did with the Contactees. It probably gets a lot of help from our own brains, and our own unconscious expectations, of how it should appear to us, too.

> It involves something outside of the power structure; and the people inside the power structure probably don't like that, which is probably one of the main reasons why there has been military interest in UFOs. Whatever it is—real aliens, something like

Persinger's theories, DMT, or something from somewhere else entirely—it was screaming to the Contactees, and it's still screaming to us saying: 'Pay attention here.' Maybe that's what important, and what the Contactees and the Space-Brothers, or whatever they were, were trying to tell us: pay attention, listen, learn and evolve (Bishop, 2005).

Resources

During the course of researching and writing this book, the following sources were consulted.

Introduction
Unidentified Flying Objects and Air Force Project Blue Book, U.S. Air Force
    Fact Sheet 95-03.
The FBI's UFO Files, *www.fbi.gov*
Palmer, Ray, and Arnold, Kenneth, *The Coming of the Saucers*, Amherst
    Press, 1952.

Chapter 1: Early Encounters
Letter from Walter Winchell to the FBI, July 9, 1949.
Letter from "Mr. Jones" to Walter Winchell, July 7, 1949.
Unidentified Flying Objects: *www.fbi.gov*
Fry, Daniel, *The White Sands Incident*, Horus House Press, Inc., 1992.

Challenor, James, *From the Stars?* (publication-pending), 2001.

White Sands Missile Range: *www.wsmr.army.mil/wsmr.asp*

Aerojet: *www.aerojet.com/home.php*

Daniel Fry Dot Com: *www.danielfry.com*

Sanders, Jacqueline, *The Case of Dan Fry, Saucerian*, No. 5. 1955.

Understanding Incorporated – History, Present Status, Future Objectives, Understanding, Inc., 1959.

"Centralian Tells Strange Tale of Visiting Venus Space Ship in Eastern Lewis County, Centralia Daily Chronicle," April 1, 1950.

Clark, Jerome, *The UFO Encyclopedia: The Phenomenon from the Beginning, Volume 2*, Omnigraphics, 1998.

Samuel Eaton Thompson: *http://en.wikipedia.org/wiki/Samuel_Eaton_Thompson*

Redfern, Nick, An Early Contactee:
www.ufomystic.com/the-redfern-files/an-early-contactee

Nude Aliens and the Forgotten Contactee, Cabinet of Wonders:
www.wunderkabinett.co.uk/damndata/index.php?/ archives/908-Nude-Aliens-and-the-Forgotten-Contactee.html

Chapter 2: The Ultimate Contactee

Leslie, Desmond, and Adamski, George, *Flying Saucers Have Landed*, Werner Laurie, 1953.

Adamski, George, *Behind the Flying Saucer Mystery*, Paperback Library, Inc., 1967.

Adamski, George, *Pioneers of Space*, Inner Light/Global Communications, 2008.

Zinsstag, Lou and Good, Timothy, *George Adamski—The Untold Story*, Ceti Publications, 1983.

Bennett, Colin, *Looking for Orthon*, Paraview Press, 2001.

"Shamanistic Order to be Established Here, LA Times," April 1934.

Bishop, Greg, *George A, George W. and those "tracks on the desert," Wake up Down There!*, Adventures Unlimited, 2000.

Interview with Colin Bennett, July 19, 2009.

Interview with Timothy Green Beckley, July 15, 2009. Beckley's Global Communications has published numerous books on the Contactee puzzle.

For more information, contact: Global Communications, Box 753, New Brunswick,NJ 08903.

Williamson, George Hunt, and Bailey, Alfred C., *The Saucers Speak!*, New Age, 1954.

Williamson, George Hunt, *Other Tongues–Other Flesh*, Forgotten Books, 2008.

Williamson, George Hunt, *Secret Places of the Lion*, Neville Spearman, 1969.

Pelley, William Dudley, *Star Guests*, Soulcraft Chapels, 1950.

George Hunt Williamson: *http://en.wikipedia.org/wiki/George_Hunt_Williamson*

Chapter 3: The FBI Takes Note

FBI files on George Adamski, 1950-1960, declassified to Nick Redfern via the terms of the Freedom of Information Act.

Interview with Jim Moseley, July 15, 2009. For more information on Moseley and his work, see: *Saucer Smear*, P.O. Box 1709, Key West, FL 33041.

Interview with Colin Bennett, July 19, 2009.

Bishop, Greg, *Interview: James Moseley, Saucer Smear "Commander" and Publisher*, *The Excluded Middle*, No, 4, 1995.

Chapter 4: Close Encounters With the Captain

Mormon Mesa: *http://www.sunsetcities.com/lostcity/mormonmesa/mormonmesa00.html*

Crockett, Arthur, and Beckley, Timothy Green, *Messages from the People of the Planet Clarion*, Inner Light Publications, 1995.

Bethurum, Truman, *The Voice of the Planet Clarion*, self-published, 1957.

Bethurum, Truman, *Facing Reality*, self-published, 1958.

Bethurum Truman, and Beckley, Timothy Green, *The People of the Planet Clarion*, Saucerian Books, 1970.

Bethurum, Truman, and Tennison, Mary Kay, *Aboard a Flying Saucer*, DeVorss & Co, 1954.

Alfvegren, Skylaire, Truman Bethurum's Call to Clarion:
  www.skylaire.com/trumanbethurumscalltoclarion.htm
Saucer Story Flew for a Time (Truman Bethurum):
  http://ufocasebook.com/saucerstory.html
Mormon Mesa: UFO Hot Bed: *www.klas-tv.com/Global/story.asp?S=4157195*

Chapter 5: Orfeo and the Aliens

Angelucci, Orfeo, *The Secret of the Saucers*, Amherst Press, 1955.
Angelucci, Orfeo, *Son of the Sun*, DeVorss & Co, 1959.
Angelucci, Orfeo, and Beckley, Timothy Green (editor), *Son of the Sun: Secret of the Saucers*, Inner Light, 2008.
Orfeo Angelucci: *http://en.wikipedia.org/wiki/Orfeo_Angelucci*
Orfeo Angelucci UFO Contactee Pictorial:
  http://hubpages.com/hub/Orfeo-Angelucci-UFO-Contactee-Pictorial
He experienced a cosmic glimpse in the spaceship: *www.galactic.no/rune/orfeo.html*
Orfeo Angelucci's Contact Story: *http://home.earthlink.net/~dexxxa/_wsn/page4.html*

Chapter 6: Rocking With Giants

FBI files on George Van Tassel, 1953–1965, declassified to Nick Redfern via the terms of the Freedom of Information Act.
Short, Robert, *Out of the Stars*, Infinity Publishing, 2003.
Van Tassel, George, *The Council of Seven Lights*, DeVorss and Co., 1958.
Van Tassel, George, *When Stars Look Down*, Kruckeberg Press, 1976.
Van Tassel, George, I *Rode a Flying Saucer!*, New Age, 1952.
Van Tassel, George, *Religion and Science Merged*, Ministry of Universal Wisdom, 1958.
Bishop, Greg, *Interview: James Moseley, Saucer Smear "Commander" and Publisher*, The Excluded Middle, No. 4, 1995.
Hamilton, William, The Original Space Channeler–George van Tassel:
  www.rense.com/general70/tass.htm

George Van Tassel: *http://en.wikipedia.org/wiki/George_Van_Tassel*
George Van Tassel's Amazing Integratron: *http://www.labyrinthina.com/rock.htm*
Integratron: *www.integratron.com*
Integratron: *http://en.wikipedia.org/wiki/Integratron*

Chapter 7: Alternative Aliens
Haines, Gerald, *CIA's Role in the Study of UFOs 1947–90*, *Studies in Intelligence*, Vol.1, No.1, Central Intelligence Agency, 1997.
Horsley, Peter, *Sounds from another Room*, Pen & Sword Books, Ltd., 1997.
Clarke, David, Roberts, Andy, *Flying Saucerers*, Heart of Albion Press, 2007.
Clarke, David, and Roberts, Andy, *Out of the Shadows*, Piatkus, 2002.
Good, Timothy, *Need to Know*, Pegasus Books, 2007.
McManners Hugh, and Ellis, Walter, *What the Alien Told the Equerrabout Prince Philip*, *The Times*, November 2, 1997.
Peter Horsley: *http://en.wikipedia.org/wiki/Peter_Horsley*
The Aetherius Society: *www.aetherius.org*
George King: *http://en.wikipedia.org/wiki/George_King_(Aetherius_Society)*

Chapter 8: "I am Diane. I come from Venus."
Mustapa, Margit, *Spaceship to the Unknown*, Vantage Press, 1960.
Mustapa, Margit, *Book of Brothers*, Vantage Press, 1963.
Clarke, David, and Roberts, Andy, *Flying Saucerers*, Heart of Albion Press, 2007.
Gibbons, Gavin, *They Rode in Space Ships*, Citadel Press, 1957.
Murphy, Simon, Mollie Thompson: Heralding the Dawn: *www.geocities.com/thesimonmurphy/mollie/index.htm*
Bishop, Greg, Mollie Thompson, "From Worlds Afar": *www.ufomystic.com/wake-up-down-there/mollie-thompson-from-worlds-afar*
Bishop, Greg, What about Female Contactees?: *www.ufomystic.com/wake-up-down-there/ufo-contactees-female/*
Lee, Regan, The Mystical Contactee Encounters of Dana Howard: Parallels to Marian Apparitions: *http://www/ufodigest.com/news/1207/danahoward2.html*

Howard, Dana, *Diane: She Came from Venus*, Regency Press, 1956.

Howard, Dana, *Vesta: The Earthborn Venusian*, Essene Press, 1959.

Chapter 9: Prince Uccelles

FBI files on Harold Berney, 1959, declassified to Nick Redfern via the
    terms of the Freedom of Information Act.

"Two Weeks on Venus," *Time*, April 15, 1957.

Chapter 10: Close Encounters of the Sexual Kind

Bowen, Charles (Editor), *The Humanoids*, Henry Regnery Company,
    1969.

Watson, Nigel, *Alien Sex 101: The Antonio Villas Boas Account*, *Fortean
    Times*, March 1999.

Villas Boas, Antonio, deposition, February 22, 1958.

Naisbitt, Michael, Interstellar Intercourse – The Abduction of Antonio
    Villas Boas: *www.ufodigest.com/news/0507/boas.html*

Melanson, Terry, Antonio Villas Boas: Abduction Episode Ground Zero:
    www.conspiracyarchive.com/UFOs/boas-abduction.htm

Menger, Howard, *From Outer Space to You*, Saucerian Books, 1959.

Bishop, Greg, Howard Menger Passes:
www.ufomystic.com/wake-up-down-there/howard-menger-passes

Chapter 11: Aho, Let's Go!

Interview with Wayne Aho, August 1998.

Wayne Sulo Aho: *http://en.wikipedia.org/wiki/Wayne_Sulo_Aho
    Crash Pad*, *Time*, July 3, 1978.

Reinhold O. Schmidt, *http://en.wikipedia.org/wiki/Reinhold_O._Schmidt*

The Claimed UFO Contacts of Reinhold Schmidt: *http://galactic.to/rune/
    reinhold.html*

Otis T. Carr and his Flying Machine: *www.keelynet.com/gravity/carr3.htm*

Shore, Ron, *Saucer Lies* (unpublished manuscript) *Saucer Smear*, April 5,
2006.

Chapter 12: E.T. Infiltration

Interview with Marion Shaw, January 9, 2009.

Stringfield, Leonard, *UFO Crash-Retrievals: Amassing the Evidence*, privately published, 1982.

Flying Saucer Review, Vol. 39, No. 3.

Lecture given by Robert Dean at the Civic Theater, Leeds, England, September 24, 1994.

FBI files on George Frank Stranges declassified to Nick Redfern via the terms of the Freedom of Information Act.

Stranges, Frank, *Stranger at the Pentagon*, I.E.C. Inc., Book Division, 1967.

Frank E. Stranges, and Valiant Thor: *www.bibliotecapleyades.net/bb/stranges*

Bishop, Greg, Frank Stranges Passes: *www.ufomystic.com/wake-up-down-there/frank-stranges-passes*

Chapter 13: Aliens on the Mountain

Western NC Attractions: *www.westernncattractions.com/BmLights.htm*

Brown Mountain (North Carolina): *http://en.wikipedia.org/wiki/Brown-Mountain-North-Carolina)*

Origin of the Brown Mountain Light in North Carolina, U.S. Geological Survey, 1922.

The Brown Mountain Lights: *www.ibiblio.org/ghosts/bmtn.html*

The Brown Mountain Lights: *www.phys.appstate.edu/caton/BML/index.htm*

The Brown Mountain Lights: *www.brownmountainlights.com*

Wolff, Linda, "Remembering Ralph Lael and the Brown Mountain Lights,"Alternate Perceptions Magazine, no. 78, April 2004.

Lael, Ralph, *The Brown Mountain Lights*, self-published, 1965.

Hanks, Micah, Ralph Lael's "Alien Muppet": Where is he now?: *http://gralienreport.com/conspiracies/ralph-laels-alien-muppet-where-is-he-now/*

Interview with Micah Hanks, July 7, 2009.

Interview with Timothy Green Beckley, July 15, 2009.

On the Trail of the Flying Saucers, Timothy Green Beckley, Issue 64, June 1969.

A Shrine to Homer Tate, "The Desert Pygmy King," Doug Higley: *http://grindshow.com/GrindShow/Shrine_Of_Homer_Tate.html*

Sideshow World, Homer Martin Tate: *www.sideshowworld.com/HTC1.html*

Chapter 14: "Believe in us, but not too much."
Sanford, Ray, *Socorro Saucer in a Pentagon Pantry*, Blueapple Books, 1976.
Steiger, Brad, *Project Blue Book*, Ballantine Books, 1976.
Studies in Intelligence, Central Intelligence Agency, 1966.
Huyghe, Patrick, *Swamp Gas Times*, Paraview Press, 2001.
FBI documentation, 1967.
Bishop, Greg, Don't Believe Too Much:
   www.ufomystic.com/wake-up-down-there/ufo-belief-abduction-schirmer/
Blum, Ralph & Blum, Judy, *Beyond Earth*, Bantam Books, 1978.
1967—The Herbert Schirmer Abduction:
   http://ufos.about.com/od/aliensalienabduction/p/schirmer.htm
Police Officer Herbert Schirmer Abduction: *www.ufoevidence.org/cases/case659.htm*
1967—The Abduction of Patrolman Herbert Schirmer:
   www.ufocasebook.com/herbertschirmer.html

Chapter 15: Saucers in the 70s
Flying Saucer Review, Vol. 26, No. 4.
Claude Vorilhon: *http://en.wikipedia.org/wiki/Claude_Vorilhon*
Vallee, Jacques, *Messengers of Deception*, Daily Grail Publishing, 2008.
Raëlism: *http://en.wikipedia.org/wiki/RA%C3%ABlism*
Website of the Raëlian Movement: *www.rael.org*
Raëlianews: *http://raelianews.org/news.php*
Raëlism: *http://neohumanism.org/r/ra/raelism.html*
Raëlian Leader Says Cloning First Step to Immortality:
   http://archives.cnn.com/2002/HEALTH/12/27/human.cloning/index.html
The First Picture of the Raëlian Clone:
   www.weeklystandard.com/Content/Public/.../071vyjdo.asp
Raël, *Intelligent Design*, Nova Distribution, 2006.
Raël, *Space Aliens Took me to Their Planet*, Edition du Message, 1978.
Raël, *The Book That Tells the Truth*, La Negrerie, 1976.
Raël, *The True Face of God*, Religion, Raelienne, 1998.
Billy Meier: *http://en.wikipedia.org/wiki/Billy_Meier*

Billy Meier's Alien Contacts: *http://crystalinks.com/billy_meier.html*

About Billy Meier: *www.steelmarkonline.com/about_billy_meier.htm*

The Future of Mankind: *http://futureofmankind.co.uk/Billy_Meier/Main_ Page*

Winters, Randolph, and Meier, Billy, *The Pleiadian Data Book*, The Pleiades Project, 1993.

Perkins, Rodney, and Jackson, Forrest, *Cosmic Suicide*, Pentaradial Press, 1997.

Henry, William, *The Keepers of Heaven's Gate*, Earthpulse Press, 1997.

Heaven's Gate (religious group): *http://en/wikipedia.org/wiki/Heaven's_Gate_(religious_group)*

Chapter 16: Circles and Space-Brothers

Dog Walker Met "UFO" Alien with Scandinavian Accent, Sarah Knapton, *Daily Telegraph*, March 22, 2009.

Interviews with Vanessa Martin, July 4 and July 10, 2008.

Mizrach, Steve, Thunderbird and Trickster, *www.fiu.edu/~mizrachs/thunderbird-and-trickster.html*

Heyoka: *www.redelk.org/website/heyoka.htm*

Wallis, Wilson D., *Heyoka: Rites of Reversal*, Lakota Books, 1996.

Interview with Colin Bennett, July 19, 2009.

Hanks, Micah: Circular Evidence: Crop Circles and High Strangeness in the UK: *http://gralienreport.com/ufos/circular-evidence-crop-circles-and-high-strangeness-in-the-uk*

Chapter 17: Altered States

Hypnagogia: A Bridge to Other Realities: *http://serendip.brynmawr.edu/exchange/node/1800*

Consciousness and Hypnagogia: *www.world-of-lucid-dreaming.com/consciousness-and-hypnagogia.html*

Short, Robert, *Out of the Stars*, Infinity Publishing, 2003.

Hiddell, Alec, "Tracks in the Desert," *The Excluded Middle*, No. 3, 1995.

Pickover, Clifford A., *Sex, Drugs, Einstein & Elves*, Smart Publications, 2005.

DMT: The Spirit Molecule: *www.thespiritmolecule.com*
Overview: *http://rickstrassman.com/dmt/*
Hanks, Micah, What Hails from Beyond: Shamanic Drugs, or
Pathways to Other Dimensions?: *http://gralienreport.com/fortean-*
phenomena/what-hails-from-beyond-shamanic-drugs-or-pathways-to-other-
dimensions/
Bishop, Greg, online interview with Richard Strassman:
    www.ufomystic.com/wake-up-down-there/interview-richard-
    strassman-dmt- abductions/
Bishop, Greg, Drugs and UFO Abductions Update:
    http://www.ufomystic.com/wake-up-down-there/alien-abduction-
    dmt-drugs-strassman/
Bishop, Greg, Aliens and Drugs:
    http://www.ufomystic.com/wake-up-down-there/aliens-and-drugs/
Interview with Adam Gorightly, June 9, 2009.
Letter from Adam Gorightly to Jenny Randles, December 12, 1986.
Dr. Fong's House of Mysteries—Terence McKenna's Fake Flying Saucer:
    http://drfong.blogspot.com/2009/01/terence-mckennas-fake-flying-
    saucer.html
The Joseph Smith Papers: *www.josephsmithpapers.org/Default.htm*
Joseph Smith, Jr.: *http://enwikipedia.org/wiki/Joseph_Smith,_Jr.*
Fraser, Gordon, *Joseph and the Golden Plates*, Industrial Litho, 1978.

Chapter 18: Space Aliens or Secret Agents?
Bethurum, Truman, and Tennison, Mary Kay, *Aboard a Flying Saucer*,
DeVorss & Co, 1954.
Saucer News, June-July, 1955.
Interview with Jim Moseley, July 15, 2009.
Moseley, James W. and Pflock, Karl T., *Shockingly Close to the Truth*.
    Prometheus Books, 2002.
Special Branch files on George King and the Aetherius Society.
Clarke, David & Roberts, Andy, *Flying Saucerers*, Heart of Albion Press, 2007.
Davenport, Elaine, Eddy, Paul & Hurwitz, Mark, *The Hughes Papers*,
    Sphere Books, Ltd, 1977.

Andrews, George, *Extra-Terrestrials Among Us*, Llewellyn Publications, 1986.

Stringfield, Leonard, *Situation Red: The UFO Siege*, Sphere Books, Ltd., 1978.

Keel, John, *UFOs: Operation Trojan Horse*, Souvenir Press Ltd., 1971.

Menger, Howard, *From Outer Space to You*, Saucerian Books, 1959.

Chapter 19: Manipulating the Mind
The Senate MK-Ultra Hearings, Senate Select Committee on Intelligence and the Committee on Human Resources, 1977.

The Frank Olson Murder: *www.serendipity.li/cia/olson2.htm*

Angelucci, Orfeo, *The Secret of the Saucers*, Amherst Press, 1955.

Angelucci, Orfeo, *Son of the Sun*, DeVorss & Co, 1959.

Angelucci, Orfeo and Beckley, Timothy Green (editor), *Son of the Sun: Secret of the Saucers*, Inner Light, 2008.

Marks, John D, *The Manchurian Candidate*, Times Books, 1979.

Frank Olson, *http://en.wikipedia.org/wiki/Frank_Olson*

Vallee, Jacques, *Messengers of Deception*, Daily Grail Publishing, 2008.

Chapter 20: Inventing Aliens
Interview with Rich Reynolds, June 23, 2009.

The Villas Boas Event, The UFO Reality:
> *http://ufor.blogspot.com/2006/01/villa-boas-event.html*

Bowen, Charles (Editor), *The Humanoids*, Henry Regnery Company, 1969.

Buckle, Eileen, *The Scoriton Mystery*, Neville Spearman, 1967.

Oliver, Norman, *Sequel to Scoriton*, self-published, 1968.

Chapter 21: Space-Brothers vs. Crypto-Brothers
Tonnies, Mac:
> *http://posthumanblues.blogspot.com/2006/12/cryptoterrestrial-hypothesis-has-met.html*

Tonnies, Mac:
http://posthumanblues.blogspot.com/2006/04/of-course-cryptoterrestrials-dont.html

Interview with Mac Tonnies, July 7, 2009.

Interview with Timothy Green Beckley, July 15, 2009.

Guest, E.A., *The Other Paradigm*, *Fate*, April 2005.

Chapter 22: Ghost-Lights

"Centralian Tells Strange Tale of Visiting Venus Space Ship in Eastern Lewis County," *Centralia Daily Chronicle*, April 1, 1950.

Bethurum, Truman & Tennison, Mary Kay, *Aboard a Flying Saucer*, DeVorss & Co, 1954.

Fry, Daniel, *The White Sands Incident*, Best Books, 1966.

Angelucci, Orfeo, *The Secret of the Saucers*, Amherst Press, 1955.

Angelucci, Orfeo, *Son of the Sun*, DeVorss & Co, 1959.

Angelucci, Orfeo and Beckley, Timothy Green (editor), *Son of the Sun: Secret of the Saucers*, Inner Light, 2008.

Lee, Regan, The Mystical Contactee Encounters of Dana Howard:

Parallels to Marian Apparitions: *www/ufodigest.com/news/1207/danahoward2.html*

Lael, Ralph, *The Brown Mountain Lights*, self-published, 1965.

Wolff, Linda, *Remembering Ralph Lael and the Brown Mountain Lights*, *Alternate Perceptions Magazine*, no. 78, April 2004.

Interview with Timothy Green Beckley, July 15, 2009.

Short, Robert, *Out of the Stars*, Infinity Publishing, 2003.

Interview with Matthew Williams, July 28, 2006.

Flying Saucerery Presents...The Real UFO Project: *www.uk-ufo.org/condign/*

Clarke, David and Gary Anthony, "The British MOD Study: Project Condign," *International UFO Reporter*, Vol. 30, No. 4.

Little, Dr. Greg, *The Brown Mountain, NC Lights Videotaped: A Field Observation –July 2003*, *Alternate Perceptions Magazine*, Issue 70, July 2003.

Temporal Lobe: *http://en.wikipedia.org/wiki/Temporal_lobe*

Devereux, Paul: *Seeing the Light*, *Fortean Times*, No. 218, January 2007.

Evans-Wentz, W.Y., *The Fairy Faith in Celtic Countries*, New Page Books, 2004.

Vallee, Jacques, *Passport to Magonia*, Neville Spearman, 1970.

Steiger, Brad, *Beyond Shadow World*, Anomalist Books, 2009.

Dreamachine: *http://en.wikipedia.org/wiki/Dreamachine*

Interview with Micah Hanks, May 12, 2009.
Warren, Joshua P., *Pet Ghosts*, New Page Books, 2006.
Orb (optics): *http://en/wikipedia.org/wiki/Orb_(optics)*
Randle, Kevin, The Schirmer Abduction, A Different Perspective: *http://kevinrandle.blogspot.com/2008/10/schirmer-abduction.html*

Conclusions
Interview with Colin Bennett, July 19, 2009.
Interviews with Greg Bishop March 22, 2005 and June 23, 2009.

Index

About the Author

Nick Redfern is the author of many books on UFOs, cryptozoology, unexplained phenomena, and conspiracy-theories, including *Memoirs of a Monster Hunter*, *Strange Secrets*, and *Body Snatchers in the Desert*. He writes regularly for *Fortean Times*, *UFO Magazine*, and *Paranormal Magazine*. Nick lives in Arlington, Texas, and can be contacted at his Website: *www. nickredfern.com*.

Other Great Titles

Cosmic Conversations
Dialogues on the Nature of the Universe and the Search for Reality
Stephan Martin
EAN 978-1-60163-077-3
$16.99

The Resonance Key
Exploring the Links Between Vibration, Consciousness, and the Zero Point Grid
Marie D. Jones and Larry Flaxman
EAN 978-1-60163-056-8
$15.99

COMING SOON

11:11 The Time Prompt Phenomenon
The Meaning Behind Mysterious Signs, Sequences, and Synchronicities
Marie D. Jones and Larry Flaxman
EAN 978-1-60163-047-6
$15.99

Crash: When UFOs Fall From the Sky
A History of Famous Incidents, Conspiracies, and Cover-Ups
Kevin D. Randle, PhD.
EAN 978-1-60163-100-8
$16.99

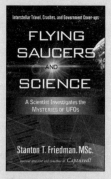

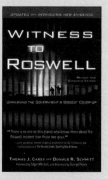
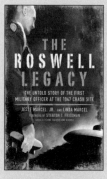